Newcastle

THE ST JAMES'S PARK ENCYCLOPEDIA

Other titles available in the same series

The Anfield Encyclopedia: an A–Z of Liverpool FC
The Old Trafford Encyclopedia: an A–Z of Manchester United FC
The Highbury Encyclopedia: an A–Z of Arsenal FC
The Elland Road Encyclopedia: an A–Z of Leeds United FC
The Stamford Bridge Encyclopedia: an A–Z of Chelsea FC
The Maine Road Encyclopedia: an A–Z of Manchester City FC
The White Hart Lane Encyclopedia: an A–Z of Tottenham Hotspur FC
  (forthcoming)

THE
ST JAMES'S PARK
ENCYCLOPEDIA

An A-Z of Newcastle United FC

Paul Harrison

*Best
Wishes
Lew
[signature]*

MAINSTREAM
PUBLISHING
EDINBURGH AND LONDON

First published in Great Britain in 1995 by
MAINSTREAM PUBLISHING COMPANY
(EDINBURGH) LTD
7 Albany Street
Edinburgh EH1 3UG

ISBN 1 85158 750 0

A catalogue record for this book is available from the British
Library

Typeset in Janson by Litho Link Ltd, Welshpool, Powys, Wales
Printed and bound in Great Britain by Butler & Tanner, Frome

To Ian Oliver –
what Newcastle United is all about

INTRODUCTION AND ACKNOWLEDGMENTS

Welcome to *The St James's Park Encyclopedia*. Newcastle United is one of the greatest British clubs of all time: a club steeped in history and one of the most successful in domestic competitions.

Whilst this encyclopedia makes no claims to be complete – such a work would take many volumes – I have tried to include as much as is feasible. Every effort has been made to ensure that statistical records are as accurate as possible. Attendance records include competitive matches only, and not wartime or secondary pre-season competitions.

This work has been a pleasure to research and write. I confess that at times I found myself virtually reliving the action played out by many of those included herein. Newcastle United are a huge club; the fanaticism of its support is as evident today as it was 100 years ago. This A to Z will, I hope, go a long way to help recall the glorious times.

It goes without saying that no book of this sort could be written without the assistance of many others, not least Newcastle United AFC Ltd. My grateful appreciation must also go to the Association of Football Statisticians; the Premier League; the Football League; the staff of the British Newspaper Library, Colindale; the staff of the Newcastle Chronicle and Journal Ltd; John Gibson and Paul Joannou for their outstanding contributions in this field prior to my own work (see Bibliography); John Robinson of Soccer Bookshelf fame; Mike Capps of KAPPA Sports Pictures, Kettering, who can supply copies of the illustrations in this book, and to every Newcastle United supporter and genuine football fan everywhere.

SELECT BIBLIOGRAPHY

John Gibson – *The Newcastle United Story (parts 1, 2, 3)* Pelham. A brilliant series of books of outstanding value to all United fans.

Paul Joannou – *United: the First Hundred Years* (ACL Polar). Quite simply this has to be one of the best books ever written about the club.

Paul Harrison – *The Elland Road Encyclopedia* (Mainstream)

Stephen F Kelly – *The Anfield Encyclopedia* (Mainstream)

Jack Rollin – *Soccer Who's Who* (Guinness)

Rothmans Football Yearbooks 1970–1994.

The above are all recommended reading. Whilst United have a virtual library of books to themselves, many are now out of print and are thus difficult to obtain. For a full list see Paul Joannou's excellent *First Hundred Years* bibliography. Countless newspapers and periodicals were further researched including Charles Buchan's *Football Monthly*, *Soccer Star*, and *The Footballer*. (For more info on Kevin Keegan see issue for October/November 1994 by Paul Joannou.)

ABANDONED. A unique incident in the club's long history occurred on 21 December 1894 when United travelled to the West Midlands to face Walsall Swifts in a League Division 2 fixture. Swifts failed to emerge from the dressing-room until some 20 minutes after the designated kick-off time. The playing staff were in dispute with the management over financial irregularities in their pay. This situation had led to strike action. After much deliberation the game went ahead, but after 78 minutes, with daylight fading and there being no floodlights, the referee had no choice but to abandon the game with Newcastle leading 3–2. The result stood and, not surprisingly, Swifts were relegated at the end of the season, to be replaced by Loughborough Town.

ADAIR, JACK. Jack Adair was the referee who awarded the penalty that almost cost United the Inter Cities Fairs Cup in 1969. The semi-final of the competition had paired United with Rangers. A two-legged affair, the first game took place in the intimidating surroundings of Ibrox Stadium, Glasgow. The date was 14 May 1969, and some 12,000 Magpies fans filled one end of the ground. The atmosphere was electric.

In the early exchanges Newcastle were well on top until there occurred an incident which is still debated in both cities to this very day. In the 34th minute Rangers' Dave Smith split the United defence with a fine lobbed-through ball. Orjan Persson, a Swede from the home side, chased after it. McFaul, the United keeper, ran from his goal in an effort to beat Persson to the bouncing ball. The crowd held their breath as both men careered towards each other. Within a split second it was all over. McFaul, fists to the fore to punch the ball clear, missed and took Persson right out of the situation, who dropped like a lead weight. The Ibrox crowd screamed 'Penalty!'. Referee Adair had no doubts. He blew his whistle and pointed to the spot: penalty to Rangers. McFaul's blow, which he later claimed to have been accidental, would have felled a raging bull. It was now down to him to defend his error.

Up stepped Andy Penman, reputed to have the hardest shot in Scottish football. Ibrox fell silent as he ran up to the ball. Penman hammered the ball to McFaul's right. It looked a goal all the way – indeed a small section of the crowd began rejoicing immediately. This turned to tears of sorrow as McFaul launched himself towards the ball. In a lunging dive, he made contact and turned the ball round for a corner. The Black 'n' White army behind the keeper's goal erupted into instant celebration. Jack Adair, the man whose decision could have turned the tie, was the first to congratulate McFaul. His name is still familar on Tyneside and in Glasgow.

AGNEW, WILLIAM. A full-back signed from the Scottish club side, Kilmarnock, in 1902, Agnew never lived up to expectations. A solid defender in Scotland, he made several nervous performances in his 44-game career at St James's Park. A return to his native country saw him progress to make 3 full international appearances for Scotland in 1907–08.

AITKEN, ANDREW. Signed for United in July 1895 as a raw but very talented 18-year-old striker, Aitken made his first-team debut against Loughborough Town, scoring a goal in his new side's 3–2 victory.

Aitken was first spotted by United scouts whilst playing for the Scottish side, Ayr Parkhouse (forerunner to Ayr United). Interest in his talent had been great, with Newton Heath (who were later renamed Manchester United) and Preston North End both attempting to lure him away from Scotland. It was Newcastle who eventually got him to sign and he became an instant terrace idol: his integrity and desire to win enamoured him to every United fan who saw him jinking around opponents with the ball. Within four years he was the team captain and went on to play for the club in every outfield position. He also made 8 full international appearances for Scotland, although it was some disappointment to him that he never scored for his country.

In all he made a total of 349 appearances for United, scoring 42 goals. In October 1906 he was sold to Middlesbrough as player/manager, where he inspired the team to a safe position in the First Division. He left Boro after a boardroom bust-up and joined East Midlands side, Leicester Fosse, where, incredibly, he gained further international honours. By 1910–11 he was back in Scotland with Dundee, later joining Kilmarnock where injury forced him to retire from playing the game he loved. He went on to manage Gateshead Town before settling on Tyneside to run a pub. In his later years he also acted as a talent scout for United. Andy Aitken was a loyal professional and a United player through and through.

AITKEN, ROY. Roy Aitken was a surprise signing by United, who profited from the big man's varied experience. Born in Irvine, Scotland, Aitken made it into the professional game with Celtic before joining Newcastle in 1989. At Celtic he had won six Championships and was a five-time Scottish Cup winner.

A fee of £500,000 secured his services for Newcastle and raised more than a few eyebrows, especially as Aitken was over 30 years of age. Those who scoffed were later to regret their apprehensions as the Scot revelled in the challenge and shone in the United line-up. His power, control and awareness made him stand out above the rest.

11

His stay on Tyneside was short-lived; just two seasons in which he made 65 appearances and scored only once, against Barnsley on 3 March 1990. He added to his international honours gaining a further 6 Scottish caps, making a total of 57 in all.

He transferred to St Mirren in 1991 where he continued to dictate on the pitch and won more international recognition before moving to Aberdeen in 1992. When Willie Miller was sacked as manager early in 1995, Aitken took over and successfully avoided relegation.

AITKEN, WILLIAM. Billy Aitken was a £2,500 capture from Rangers in the 1920–21 season. A consistent goalscorer in Scotland, United saw him as the ideal striking partner for Stan Seymour and Tom McDonald.

Aitken proved a real asset. His innovative style and sheer skill often gave the impression that the ball was stuck to his foot as he weaved in and out of the opposition, often leaving defenders on their backsides. During his four-season spell at St James's Park he made 110 appearances and scored ten goals.

ALBERT, PHILIPPE. A tall, elegant defender, Philippe Albert shone for Belgium in the 1994 World Cup, and was signed for Newcastle from RCS Anderlecht in August 1994 for a fee of £2,650,000. Albert was voted Belgian Player of the Year in 1992 and is widely regarded as one of the best defenders in the world. Already something of a crowd favourite on Tyneside, he looks set to fulfil all United's expectations.

ALDERSON, STUART. A forward who signed up as a professional for United via the amateur side, Evenwood, it was unfortunate that Alderson arrived at the club when several quality forwards were already on the books. As a result, he made just three appearances (without a goal). He seemed to lack the physical commitment required to break into the first team, and in June 1967 was transferred to York City.

ALLAN, STANLEY. A squad player between 1908 and 1911, Allan was a half-back who, with a little improvisation, was transformed into a centre-forward. In his three-year spell at the club he made 15 first-team starts and scored five goals, a reasonable return for so few games.

ALLCHURCH, IVOR. Ivor Allchurch, the Welsh Wizard, was signed from Swansea in October 1958 for a fee of around £28,000. He was a delightful footballer and, although 30 years of age when he joined Newcastle, his football knowledge and education allowed him to play rather than run. His colleagues nicknamed him the 'nearly' man, because his accurate shooting prowess was second to none: his long-range efforts would fly towards the opponents' goal as Allchurch 'nearly' always scored. He made a total of 14 international appearances for Wales whilst with the club. He donned the United colours on 154 occasions, scoring 51 goals.

In 1962 he left Newcastle and returned to Wales to play for Cardiff City, where he continued to thrill crowds at Ninian Park. On his retirement from the game he was awarded the MBE for outstanding playing services. His brother, Len, also forged a professional career in the game.

ALLEN, GEOFF. Having progressed through the United youth policy of the 1960s. Geoff Allen joined his home-town club on a professional basis in February 1964, aged just 18. He was a winger who appeared to be languishing in the reserves for a long time, lacking the confidence to sustain a challenge for regular first-team football.

Allen eventually broke through and, in an Inter-Cities Fairs Cup tie versus Feyenoord, played his greatest match ever. United won the tie 4–0 and had it not been for Allen's skilful and sensible running down the flanks and accurate crossing, victory may never have happened. Allen matured that night: he was a revelation and received a standing ovation from the United crowd. So free with his crosses and passing, Allen almost grabbed a goal himself when a rasping drive rattled against the crossbar.

In October 1968, just when everything seemed to be turning in his favour, he sustained an injury which was to force him out of the game at just 21 years of age. In all he made 26 first-team appearances and scored just once. He also achieved youth international honours for England.

ALLEN, JACK. Arrived at St James's Park in June 1931 from Sheffield Wednesday in a £35,000 transfer deal. Jack Allen had originally been spotted some years earlier playing for Prudhoe Castle Juniors, from where Leeds United signed him in 1924. He later had a spell at Brentford, before heading north to join Wednesday, where he proved himself to be a prolific goalscorer. His Newcastle debut was not a good one – he missed a penalty against Portsmouth. But the player put this behind him and went on to score 41 goals from 90 United appearances. Two of his most important strikes brought the FA Cup to St James's Park in April 1932, when United beat Arsenal 2–1.

ALLEN, MALCOLM. Signed by Kevin Keegan in a £300,000 swoop on Millwall, Malcolm Allen is an old-fashioned centre-forward, raiding opposing defences and snapping up half chances. He is a player with an uncanny knack of being in the right place at the right time – as with a goal against Sheffield Wednesday in the 1993–94 season: an aimless ball into the box, a sweet nod of Allen's head – and it's a goal! Allen is the kind of player who will score goals wherever he plays.

ALLEN, RONALD. Right-winger with previous League experience at Dundee and Preston. Scored four goals in 29 appearances for Newcastle in the 1897–98 season. A quiet Scot who was a great asset in United's bid for promotion that season.

ALLON, JOE. Progressed through the youth team to make his debut against Sheffield Wednesday in 1986–87, where he promptly scored in a 2–0 victory. Everything seemed set for the local lad, born in Gateshead, to become a new legend. But it all went wrong. An undoubted scorer of goals,

Allon's career never took off and most people will remember him because of his distinctive blond hair rather than any football achievements. He only managed ten games at Newcastle, scoring twice. Transferred to Swansea City in 1987–88, he later played for Hartlepool United, Chelsea and Brentford. A genuine lad, he seemed to lose his way amidst the high-profile attentions of the media at the time.

ANCELL, ROBERT. The Dumfries-born Ancell had a number of English clubs chasing him when he was in the St Mirren line-up. Newcastle narrowly beat Carlisle United in 1936 in the race to win the skilful defender's signature. As well as gaining two caps for Scotland, Ancell played 102 matches for Newcastle (plus 53 Wartime League games) without scoring.

ANDERSON, ANDREW. Yet another signing from St Mirren, Andy Anderson was an out-and-out left-winger with bags of pace and a deft touch. Initially purchased as a squad player, he proved to be so much more than that. He made 67 first-team appearances, scoring seven goals, and was a member of the successful 1908–9 Championship-winning side.

ANDERSON, JOHN. 'Ando' was a great crowd favourite and a leader amongst his peers. An honest, genuine Irishman, he was signed from Preston North End, having previously been with West Bromwich Albion. Incredibly, Anderson was freed by Preston and came to Newcastle with something to prove – and prove it he did. Some 322 appearances (with 17 more as a substitute) and 15 goals later, he can claim to have outlasted four different managers! He collected 11 international caps for the Republic of Ireland whilst at the club. Anderson's signing was perhaps one of the best deals ever made at St James's Park.

ANDERSON, STANLEY. Born in Horden in 1934, Stan Anderson joined Sunderland in October 1952. Regarded as a midfield terrier with an eye for goal, United signed him in

November 1963, where his leadership qualities were recognised and he was quickly made team captain.

Described as a 'gentleman', Anderson was, where football matters were concerned, a strong and forceful character. He took United to the Second Division Championship in 1965 and made a total of 84 appearances for the Magpies, scoring 14 goals, before being sold to Middlesbrough. He made two full international appearances for England, and four U-23 appearances. A sending-off against Bulgaria seriously hampered the development of his international career, as thereafter he was regarded as being quick-tempered.

Unique in as much as he has captained Newcastle, Sunderland and Middlesbrough, Anderson found management much more difficult. First he took over at Boro, then Doncaster, Bolton Wanderers, and AEK Athens.

ANGLO-ITALIAN CUP. A pre-season tournament in which United have participated twice. The first time was in 1972–73 when competition results went as follows:
Roma (a) won 2–0 (Tudor 2)
Bologna (h) won 1–0 (Gibb)
Como (a) won 2–0 (Moncur, Tudor)
Torino (h) won 5–1 (Tudor, Gibb, Macdonald, Hibbitt, o.g.)
Semi-final: **Crystal Palace** (a) draw 0–0; **Crystal Palace** (h) won 5–1 (Macdonald 3, Gibb, Barrowclough)
Final: **AC Fiorentina** (a) won 2–1 (Gibb, o.g.)
Newcastle United were the winners.

The second campaign was in 1992–93 and was slightly less glorious:
Grimsby Town (a) draw 2–2 (Quinn, Kelly)
Leicester City (h) won 4–0 (Quinn 2, Brock, Sheedy)
Luchesse (a) draw 1–1 (Kristensen)
Ascoli (h) lost 1–0
Bari (a) lost 3–0
Cesena (h) draw 2–2 (Peacock 2)
In the final Cremonese beat Derby County 3–1.

ANGLO-SCOTTISH CUP. Replacing the Watneys and the Texaco Cup, this was a pre-season tournament which generally involved Scottish clubs and selected First and Second Division sides from England. As a result, local derbies were frequent events:

1975–76: **Carlisle United** (a) lost 2–0
Sunderland (h) lost 2–0
Middlesbrough (h) draw 2–2 (Hibbitt, Gowling)

The following season was not much better:
1976–77: **Sheffield United** (a) won 1–0 (Gowling)
Hull City (a) drew 0–0
Middlesbrough (h) won 3–0 (Gowling 2, Barrowclough)
Ayr United (a) lost 3–0

This last fixture was supposed to be over two legs. However, United fielded such a weakened side in the first leg that the competition authorities had no option but to disqualify them, awarding the tie to Ayr United!

APPEARANCES. The record number of appearances made by any player for Newcastle United stands at 505 games, the total notched up by Jimmy Lawrence between 1904 and 1922. He played 432 League games, 64 FA Cup ties, and made nine Wartime League appearances.

APPLEBY, MATTHEW. Another youth-team product, Appleby was a promising defender who appeared to be heading for a long career at St James's Park. Signed in 1990, he made 25 first-team outings, with a further five as a substitute. Many people were shocked to learn that Kevin Keegan had allowed him to leave the club on a free transfer to Darlington in 1994.

Appleby has a younger brother, Ritchie, who is also on United's books, as a midfielder.

APPLEYARD, WILLIAM. Signed at the end of the 1902–3 season from Grimsby Town, Bill Appleyard had impressed the United management in a previous season's FA Cup encounter between the two clubs. In a five-year spell on Tyneside Appleyard scored 87 goals, many crucial or sensational, which endeared him to the hearts of the devout

United following. In the Championship-winning season of 1905 he weighed in with 13 goals. Appleyard was without doubt one of the first 'super strikers' in the club's history. He made a total of 145 appearances for the Magpies.

ARDILES, OSVALDO. Ossie came to Newcastle in March 1991 as a replacement for the 'Bald Eagle', Jim Smith. He was manager of Swindon Town at the time, and United had to pay out a sum of £160,000 in compensation to assure his services from the Wiltshire club.

Ardiles, the player, was exciting and he had a glorious career. Ardiles, the manager, was a totally different proposition. He landed a financially lucrative three-year deal on Tyneside but lasted little more than 12 months. Aware of the club's fanatical support, he attempted to instil his own brand of football in far too short a space of time. Out went the ageing stars to be replaced by promising youngsters who had played most of their football in the reserves or in the lower leagues. It was all too hasty. Yes, everyone longed for success to return, but Ossie wanted it yesterday. The first-team line-up changed virtually every week and eventually injuries and suspensions began to take their toll. Results were, to say the least, terrible. Things got so bad that United were now filling a relegation slot. It was clear that something had to be done – and so, Ossie was sacked.

He moved on to manage West Bromwich Albion, where he later resigned to take over at Tottenham Hotspur. Sacked again in 1994 with the London club giving away goals at an alarming rate, Ossie has earned the sympathy of everyone on Tyneside. His ideas were right, but he failed to blend youth with experience. If he had opted for this approach, who knows what he could have achieved.

ARENTOFT, PREBEN. Born in Denmark in 1942, Ben Arentoft joined United from Morton in March 1969. A solid, well-built midfielder with a big heart, he was alert, enthusiastic and bright in his manner both on and off the field. He was a major contributor to the successful Fairs Cup campaign of 1969. In the second leg of the final in

Budapest he volleyed home a cracking second equaliser which all but killed off Ujpesti's challenge. As part of the victorious United team, Arentoft became the first-ever overseas player to win a European competition winner's medal with a British club. Incredibly, that goal was one of just three he scored in his time at Newcastle before being sold to Blackburn Rovers in September 1971. Arentoft made a total of 59 appearances, with a further five as a substitute.

ASKEW, WILLIAM. Billy Askew started his football career as an apprentice at Middlesbrough, where he made ten appearances, before transferring to Hull City in September 1982. He joined Newcastle in 1990 but managed just seven appearances, with a further one on the substitutes' bench. Released by Ossie Ardiles, Askew was a good-mannered individual who never really had the opportunity to prove himself at St James's Park.

ATTENDANCE. The record attendance at St James's Park for a League fixture stands at 68,386 v Chelsea on 3 September 1930. United won the match 1–0. This is the 12th biggest Football League attendance in English records. Receipts on the day were also a club record at £4,267, 0s 8d.

A further English attendance record was set at St James's Park on 14 February 1948 when United faced Liverpool in a non-competitive fixture. The game was arranged as part of a deal which saw United star Albert Stubbins transfer to the then League Champions. A crowd of 44,840, the biggest ever between two English club sides in a friendly fixture, turned out to witness a Liverpool victory by three goals to nil. For the record, Albert Stubbins missed a penalty for his new club and was subjected to playful taunts from the home fans!

AULD, JOHN. There can be few footballers who sign for a club and are later appointed to the official board of directors, but John Auld is one such player. He also has a further distinction to his credit, namely being the first-ever player to be transferred from Sunderland to United. A

Scottish international whilst playing for Third Lanark, Auld made just 15 appearances for United and scored three goals before his move 'upstairs'. His playing days were limited at Newcastle to the 1896–97 season.

B

BAILEY, JOHN. A Liverpool-born full-back who began his career at Blackburn Rovers in July 1975. Moving to Everton four years later, Bailey eventually joined United in 1985, playing in 41 first-team games and appearing once as a substitute. Although he gave the appearance of being overweight, Bailey was solid and reliable but often clumsy on the ball. He remained at St James's Park for just three seasons, moving to Bristol City in the 1988–89 season.

BAIRD, IAN. A strong, lively forward who joined Newcastle for a loan spell in 1984–85, Baird made five appearances and scored in a 2–1 defeat at West Bromwich Albion. Something of a football nomad, Ian joined Leeds (twice), Portsmouth, Middlesbrough, Heart of Midlothian and Bristol City – all by the age of 30! His clubs prior to his loan spell on Tyneside were Southampton (twice) and Cardiff City.

BARBER, STANLEY. Joined the United squad during a massive rebuilding period. Barber played just one game after his transfer from nearby Wallsend in 1925. He stayed at Newcastle for three seasons before being released.

BARKER, MICK. Born in Bishop Auckland, Barker joined United as an apprentice. As a defender, he made 27 appearances and a further two as a substitute before being transferred to Gillingham in January 1979.

BARR, W. A squad player who was unable to stake a claim for a regular first-team spot during United's debut season in the Football League, making a solitary appearance for the club. One of several players of the era who came and went as United dabbled with local talent in an effort to sign quality players.

BARROWCLOUGH, STEWART. A Yorkshire-born midfielder of undoubted talent, Barrowclough joined his local side, Barnsley, in 1969 before moving to Newcastle in August 1970. A slenderly built player, Barrowclough quickly broke into the first team and made the midfield role his own. He was never outclassed and was bitterly disappointed to be left out of the 1974 Cup final side. A model professional, he went on to make 201 first-team appearances with a further 18 as a substitute, scoring 20 goals. He won five England U-23 caps. He was transferred to Birmingham City in 1978.

BARTLETT, T. Made three appearances in two separate spells with the club. Joined in 1893–94 but was released, only to return in 1896–97 when he made all his United appearances. Bartlett scored three goals whilst in United colours.

BARTON, DAVID. A local defender who made 101 first-team appearances between 1977 and 1981, Barton progressed through the apprentice ranks. He made further appearances as a substitute and scored five goals. He was sold to Blackburn Rovers in August 1982.

BARTON, WARREN. Kevin Keegan signed Warren Barton from Wimbledon in the summer of 1995 for an incredible £4.5 million. Born in London, Barton began his career with Leytonstone/Ilford, before moving on to Maidstone in

1989. He made 42 League appearances at Maidstone before his transfer to Wimbledon. There, he quickly established himself as one of the best defenders in the English game, attracting not only the attentions of the country's top managers but also the eye of England coach Terry Venables. Now a fully-fledged international, the solid and reliable Barton will undoubtedly repay Keegan's investment in him.

BASTIA. UEFA Cup opponents in the 1977–78 season when two poor performances saw United ousted from the trophy: a 2–1 defeat away from home was followed by a 3–1 reversal at home. United's goals were scored by Cannell and Gowling.

BATTY, RON. A full-back who joined United from East Tanfield Colliery, Batty played alongside some of the United greats and did not look out of place. Mr Dependable, he made 181 League appearances and scored just once. In March 1958 he transferred to Gateshead. Batty was one of the unsung heroes of a great Newcastle side. He was with United between 1945 and 1958.

BEARDSLEY, PETER. A player of supreme quality, Peter Beardsley is one of the United all-time greats. His career began at Carlisle United in August 1979. He was a local lad destined to join his favourites. He arrived in 1983 and played some 203 games, scoring 85 times, with one further appearance as a substitute. Beardsley would jink one way, then the other, leaving the opposition in his wake. The diminutive striker-cum-midfielder possessed talent not seen on Tyneside for many years. He was a firm favourite with the fans. He left the club for Liverpool in 1987 and eventually joined Everton, before returning to his beloved Newcastle in 1993.

I recall seeing the young Beardsley playing for Carlisle United at Blackpool, where he scored one of the greatest goals ever seen at Bloomfield Road. He rounded four defenders before looping the ball into the top corner of the net. Upon seeing this, the person next to me commented: 'Bloody brilliant!' – the perfect way to sum up Peter Beardsley.

Peter Beardsley

BEASANT, DAVE. The tall, gangly keeper was a surprise signing. He made his name at Wimbledon before joining Newcastle in 1988, when he made 24 League appearances in his solitary season on Tyneside. He was prone to some horrific howlers, and many thought he possessed the flaws associated with keepers such as Leeds' Gary Sprake. On a good day he was brilliant, but bad days were very bad, and of these, there were many. He never quite proved himself in the North East yet his professionalism earned him the respect of the fans. He now plays for Southampton.

BEDFORD, HARRY. Signed from Derby County for a £4,000 fee in 1930, Bedford was an ex-England international striker. He made 32 appearances and scored 18 goals before moving from St James's Park in 1932.

BELL, ANTHONY. A goalkeeper born in North Shields, Bell signed for United in March 1973. He made a solitary appearance in 1974.

BELL, DAVID. This full-back, who struggled to find any consistency, made 23 appearances (scoring once) between 1930 and 1934. Bell eventually moved on to Derby County but was to make his name at Ipswich Town, where he notched up 146 appearances.

BELL, DEREK. Local lad who operated in the midfield – a position which United had already covered with a wealth of big-name talent – thus making it difficult for lesser players to break through. Bell did just that, but managed only three games with a further one as a substitute between 1981 and 1983.

BELL, JACKIE. A United junior who signed professional in November 1956, Jackie Bell was a giant with the ball at his feet. A wing-half, he made some 117 appearances between 1956 and 1962, scoring eight goals.

BELL, JOSEPH. As chairman of Newcastle United between 1909 and 1911 Bell oversaw some of the most successful years in the club's history. He was an enigmatic character who earned the respect of the players and club officials alike. A genuine character known to the playing squad as 'Uncle Joe'.

BENNETT, ALBERT. A centre-forward who arrived via a brief spell at Millmoor with Rotherham United. Bennett was a typical centre-forward, prepared to run for anything and everything, hustling and bustling defenders. He made one England U-23 appearance and also enjoyed Youth international honours. Between 1965 and 1969 he made 89 appearances for United, with one more as a substitute, scoring 23 goals. He had a marvellous partnership with fellow United striker Wyn Davies. Transferred to Norwich in February 1969.

BENNIE, ROBERT. Signed from St Mirren in 1901, Bennie made a total of 37 appearances for Newcastle before retiring in 1904 through a knee injury. He later became a director of the club.

BENTLEY, ROY. Arrived at United shortly after the war in June 1946 in an £8,000 transfer from Bristol City. Bentley was a centre-forward with outstanding heading ability and a powerful shot – everything you could want from a striker. Sold to Chelsea for £11,000 in January 1948, he made 48 appearances for Newcastle and scored 21 goals.

BERESFORD, JOHN. Beresford came to St James's Park in June 1992 from Second Division Portsmouth. He is an experienced defender who cost £650,000, and has thus far proved himself equal to the task before him. Comfortable on the ball, he is one of the mainstays of the side. Enjoys making those overlapping runs into the opponents' defence.

BETTON, ALEC. Came via the then unlikely source of non-League side Scarborough in 1931. Betton made 63 appearances and scored once during his time with the club, which ended in 1934.

BIRD, JOHN. Defender who signed from Preston in August 1975, Bird made an instant impact at the club and went on to play 93 matches, four as a substitute, and scored six goals between 1975 and 1980. He was then transferred to Hartlepool United.

BIRKETT, RALPH. Signed for £6,000, a club record at the time, from Arsenal, Birkett was an out-and-out goalscorer.

John Beresford

Sadly, with the outbreak of war, he was limited to just 26 Football League appearances and three goals. He did make a further 40 Wartime appearances, notching up a further 12 goals.

BLACK, JOHN. One of the main inspirations behind Newcastle West End, Black was a publican, who owned The Lord Hill close to St James's Park. In fact, the club and its players would use his pub as a dressing-room or meeting-

27

room. Black went on to become a director of the newly formed Newcastle United until 1899.

BLACKHALL, RAY. Signed in August 1978. A defender who rose through the juniors into the first team, Blackhall was eventually sold on to Sheffield Wednesday in 1978. He made 26 appearances for Newcastle and 11 more as a substitute.

BLACKLEY, JOHN. Scottish international defender brought in from Hibernian in August 1977, Blackley was almost 30 years of age when he came to the club. His lack of pace would often let him down. He was a strong character who could be a little reckless. He made 52 appearances between 1977 and 1979 before being transferred to Preston.

BLAKE, SIDNEY. Somewhat unique, Blake signed from Whitley Bay in 1905 but did not play a full first-team match until returning to the club in 1909. Blake's debut was as outside-left, which is curious as he was in fact a goalkeeper! Made 14 appearances as keeper, one as a winger. No goals!

BLANTHORNE, ROBERT. Signed for £350 from Grimsby Town in 1908 and made just one appearance for United – at Bradford City – where he broke his leg. Blanthorne was a 6'1" gangly centre-forward.

BLAYDON RACES. A song composed by George Ridley and sung in the music-halls of Newcastle. Adopted by supporters of Newcastle United as their anthem. The chorus so often heard echoing around football grounds of England currently goes as follows:

O me lads ye shud only see us gannin'
Passin the folks upon the road just as they wor stannin'
Thor wes lots o' lads and lasses thear
Or wi smilin faces
Gannin alang St James's Park
T'see Kev Keegan's aces.

The variations are innumerable, but there can be no denying the atmosphere created as the United throng burst into several choruses of 'Blaydon Races'.

BOAM, STUART. A curious signing from Middlesbrough – since United already had several tall central-defenders on their books – Boam arrived at St James's Park in August 1979. He made 77 appearances, scoring twice, before being transferred to Mansfield Town. He worked hard whilst in a black-and-white shirt.

BODIN, PAUL. Had a brief loan spell with club in the 1991–92 season. Welsh-born midfielder who never proved himself during the loan spell. Six appearances, no goals.

BOGIE, IAN. Newcastle-born midfielder who made eight League appearances and a further ten as a substitute, Bogie was a youngster who displayed potential which, sadly, only bloomed following his move to Preston in 1988–89.

BOOTH, CURTIS. Striker who made 34 League appearances for United, scoring six goals. His career was disrupted by active service with the Durham Light Infantry during the First World War.

BOTT, WILF. Outside-right signed from Huddersfield Town who made a sensational start to his United career – a hat-trick at home to Bury on his debut. Bott went on to score 14 goals in 44 appearances. One dreads to think of the songs chanted on the terraces about his name!

BOTTOM, ARTHUR. Another forward with an unfortunate name, Bottom was anything but bottom of the scoring-appearances ratio. His record in 1958 stands at 11 appearances, 10 goals. Moved to Chesterfield in November less than a year after joining United.

BOWDEN, RAYMOND. Signed from Arsenal for £5,000 in 1937, Bowden made 52 League appearances and scored six times. Once again, his was a career disrupted by the war.

BOWMAN, J. Left-winger who played in United's first-ever Football League fixture, against Arsenal, on 2 September 1893. This was his only game.

BOYD, JAMES. A marvellous right-winger signed from Edinburgh St Bernard's in 1925, Boyd thrilled crowds with his turn of speed and delightful crossing ability. His skill earned him an international cap for Scotland and he made a total of 214 appearances for United, scoring 63 goals, between 1925 and 1935. An outstanding talent of his era, some supporters insist Boyd is one of the greatest ever to play for the club.

BRACEWELL, PAUL. Having played for Stoke City, Sunderland, Everton and Newcastle, Paul Bracewell is a most experienced defender who has suffered some horrific injuries in his time. He is an England international, gaining three full caps against Germany, the United States and Nigeria. A hard-working, rock-solid player who is an inspiration to those around him.

BRADLEY, WILLIAM. As a goalkeeper, born in Jarrow, William Bradley made 143 appearances for Newcastle. One of the top keepers of his time, he was consistently good between the sticks. That he kept his position for 13 years is an indication of just how much supporters and team-mates thought of him. Bradley was unlucky never to receive international recognition.

BRANDER, GEORGE. Signed from Raith Rovers in March 1952, Brander made five appearances and scored two goals in a highly successful period for United, remaining with the club from 1952 until 1954.

BRAZIL, GARY. Apprentice at Crystal Palace before moving to Sheffield United, Port Vale, Preston and, eventually, Newcastle. Brazil was a rather clumsy forward who never really settled into United's style of play. It is doing him no discredit to state that his best performances were for lower League clubs. He made eight first-team appearances, with 18 more as a substitute, and scored three goals.

BRENNAN, FRANK. Centre-half who joined United from Airdrie in May 1946, Frank Brennan was a marvellous servant to Newcastle. His performance in the 1951 FA Cup final against Blackpool was as committed as one could hope for. Brennan did not put a foot wrong. The legendary Stan Mortenson never got a touch as Brennan out-fought, out-ran and out-played the classy striker. This was a typical Brennan performance.

Between 1946 and 1956 he made 347 appearances and scored three times, before a totally dissatisfactory split with the club, which saw his wages cut and ultimately led to his transfer. He refused to accept the decrease in his salary, was released and moved to North Shields as player/coach. The city of Newcastle was in uproar as one of its favourite sons had been let down by the club he served so well. It was sad end to a distinguished career.

BROADIS, IVOR. His career started as an amateur at Tottenham Hotspur before he signed for Carlisle United in August 1946. Broadis become player/manager of the Cumbrians and actually transferred himself to Sunderland in February 1949. After a two-year spell at Roker Park and a further two years at Manchester City, he arrived on Tyneside with a wealth of experience.

Broadis was a strong, spritely inside-forward and a capable provider for his colleagues. He often carried the workload for the United attack. He made 48 appearances and scored 18 goals on Tyneside before returning to Carlisle United.

Broadis gained international recognition – six full England caps – whilst at Newcastle. He was a class player who served each of his clubs well. Today he concentrates on sports writing for a number of northern newspapers.

BROCK, KEVIN. A solid, hard central-defender, Brock had an awesome reputation for his strong-hearted attitude on the pitch, the kind of player every supporter enjoys having in their side as very little (including players) got past him. Brock played for Oxford and QPR before joining United in 1988. He made 153 League appearances, ten more as a substitute, and scored 16 goals.

BROWN, ALAN. A Sunderland forward who made five appearances on loan for United in the 1981–82 season, scoring three goals. He later moved on to Shrewsbury Town, then Doncaster Rovers. Brown was one of those players who drifts in and out of a game; he seemed to lack the commitment required of him. Perhaps Newcastle were just too big a club for him.

BROWN, HARRY. Signed from Southampton in July 1906 for a fee of £380, Brown scored a hat-trick on his first-team debut and appeared to be a real bargain. Sadly, though, he contracted an illness which forced him to retire from the game, his eyesight being badly affected. He played 24 games and scored eight goals for United in 1906–7.

BROWN, MALCOLM. A defender who was brought to Newcastle via Bury and Huddersfield Town. He had a reputation for goalscoring and had netted nine goals in the season prior to joining United. Unfortunately, that sort of performance never followed him to Newcastle. He went on to make 45 appearances for the club – without a goal – between 1983–84 and 1985–86, before returning to Huddersfield Town.

BROWNLIE, JOHN. Hibernian defender who arrived at St James's Park in August 1978, Brownlie was a class act. However, his move to the English game saw the end of his international career. Four years after his move to England – 135 games and three goals later – he was transferred to Middlesbrough in August 1982.

BRUCE, ALEX. A forward with a huge reputation who came from Preston where he had scored seven goals in 55 games. However, Bruce always seemed out of sorts at Newcastle, and struggled to make any impact. It was a big step from Second Division to First Division football and Bruce found it very difficult.

After 16 games, four more as a substitute, and three goals, he was grateful for a move back to Preson in August 1975, where he proved himself an astute scorer with 135 goals in 288 League appearances.

BURGESS, CHARLES. In his one season at Newcastle Charles Burgess clocked up 30 first-team appearances (without a goal). Not surprising, really, as he was a solid full-back with a strong boot. 1900–1 was his only season at St James's Park.

BURLEIGH, MARTIN. Hefty goalkeeper Martin Burleigh was actually put on a diet by one of his clubs, which were all northern-based: Newcastle, Darlington, Carlisle, Darlington (again) and Hartlepool. Despite the weight problem, Burleigh was a fine shot-stopper, enjoying the dramatic, straight-forward saves which were made to appear sensational by his twisting acrobatics. This occasionally led to the odd mistake.

Burleigh was restricted to just 11 League appearances for United before his move to Darlington in October 1974.

BURNS, MICHAEL. Like so many players of the time, Burns was signed from his local club side, Chilton Colliery, in 1927. He was a goalkeeper who made 107 appearances for United between 1927 and 1936 and went on to play for Ipswich Town and Preston North End.

BURNS, MICKEY. Mickey Burns was a real footballer. A schoolboy idol, his outstanding work-rate, ball skill and eye for the game made him a very valuable asset on the field. Signed from Blackpool in July 1974, he made an instant impact with two outstanding pre-season goals at Brunton Park, Carlisle. Not the tallest of players, he made up for this with a huge heart and sheer determination. He scored 48 goals in 178 appearances. Players of Mickey Burns's class are rare, and United got the best of his flair and ingenuity before selling him to Cardiff City in 1978.

BURRIDGE, JOHN. This incredible goalkeeper, with so much love and dedication for the game, was born in Workington, West Cumbria. After playing for his home-town club 'Budgie' moved to Blackpool, Aston Villa, Southend United, Crystal Palace, QPR, Wolves, Derby County, Sheffield United and Southampton, from whom United signed him as a mere 38-year-old!

Burridge remained at Newcastle for two seasons, making 78 appearances in total. He was transferred to Edinburgh club, Hibernian, in 1991. A champion amongst goalkeepers, Budgie has few faults, apart from the fact that he occasionally goes to bed with a football in his hands!

John Burridge

BURTON, ALWYN. Quietly spoken Welshman who came to Newcastle in June 1963 after spells with Newport County and Norwich City. Ollie was a wing-half but was signed very much as a squad player. With Robert Moncur holding down the regular first-team spot, opportunities for the Welshman looked to be few and far between.

Ollie was a hard-worker and his perseverance paid off when first-team football beckoned. Once in, it was hard to shift him, as his tough tackling and wonderful passing abilities, supported by a sometimes amazing ability to outjump the tallest of centre-forwards, ensured that he was to become a crowd favourite. International honours followed, as did European success with United.

Ollie Burton went on to make 215 appearances for the club, playing a futher nine games as a substitute, and scored eight goals. A real stalwart, Burton is synonymous with the hard-working midfield United had during his time at the club.

BUSBY, VIV. A prolific goalscorer wherever he has been, Viv Busby started his football career with Wycombe Wanderers and moved to Luton Town in 1970. There followed a loan spell at Newcastle in December 1971. Busby played four games and scored twice, a reasonable return in such a short spell. He later played for Fulham, Norwich, Stoke, Sheffield United, Blackburn Rovers, York City and abroad with US side Tulsa Roughnecks.

BUTLER, JOSEPH. Signed professional after serving time in the juniors in September 1960. Butler was a Newcastle-born defender who made three appearances for the club, without scoring. He was transferred to Swindon Town in August 1965.

C

CAHILL, THOMAS. Scottish-born full-back who was signed from Vale of Leven in December 1951. He failed to break into the first team until 1952–53, when he made four appearances, without scoring. He transferred to Barrow in August 1955, where he remained for 11 years.

CAIE, ALEX. This sturdy, well-built half-back was signed from Millwall Athletic. Caie was described by the press of the day as 'extremely hard'! He made a total of 35 appearances for United between 1901 and 1903, scoring only once.

CAIRNS, WILLIAM. Billy Cairns was a diminutive striker, just 5′9″ tall, but he was like a terrier, refusing to give anything up as a lost cause. In 11 years at the club (1933–44), he made 90 appearances, scoring 53 times. He also made 23 Wartime League appearances, banging in a further 14 goals. After leaving Tyneside he moved to Gateshead then on to Grimsby Town, and continued playing until well after his 40th birthday.

CALLACHAN, RALPH. Ralph Callachan was born in Edinburgh and signed by Hearts, who sold him to

Newcastle in February 1977. Callachan was a midfielder and played 11 games for United in the 1977–78 season, including the two UEFA Cup-ties against Bohemians.

CAMERON, HUGH. An outside-right who was purchased from Torquay United in April 1951, Cameron never made the grade in the north-east and was sold to Bury in March 1952. He made just two appearances for Newcastle.

CAMERON, JAMES and JOHN. Brothers renowned for being leading lights behind the scenes in United's early days. James Cameron, originally a preacher before becoming a publican, later went on to become chairman of the club. John, meanwhile, took a position on the Football League Management Committee.

CAMPBELL, JOHN. As a striker, signed from Sunderland, Campbell made 26 appearances between 1897 and 1898 and scored 11 goals. He was later sacked by United for an infringement of club rules. He had taken over the management of a local hotel, which was seen as conflicting with his football career.

CANNELL, PAUL. A local lad who made good, Paul Cannell was a hard-working forward who made it through the juniors into the first team, signing professional in July 1972. He went on to make 63 appearances (two more as a substitute) and scored 18 goals. One of these was scored in the UEFA Cup 2–1 defeat at Bastia. When released by the club, he went on to play for Mansfield Town.

CAPE, JOHN. Outside-right signed from Carlisle United in 1939 for a fee of £1,500. Cape was an astute winger who supplied his frontmen with countless chances every game. He was also capable of scoring the odd goal himself. Between 1930 and 1934 he made 53 appearances and scored 20 times. Amazingly, the money Carlisle received for him was used to build one complete side of their Brunton Park ground.

CARLTON, WILLIAM. Signed from Washington Colliery, Carlton was a tall, elegant midfielder-cum-striker who made six appearances and scored once between 1926 and 1929.

CARNEY, STEVE. Signed in October 1979 from Blyth Spartans after some fine performances in one or two of their more renowned FA Cup runs, Carney was a defender who proved himself to be a good servant to the club.

He made 140 appearances (plus nine as a substitute) and scored once during his spell at St James's Park between 1979–1985. He later moved to Carlisle United.

CARR, FRANZ. This tricky winger, who could beat the best, came to Newcastle from Notts Forest, via loan spells at Sheffield Wednesday and West Ham. Carr was a frustrating player whose skill, pace and touch could astound, but whose final ball would often be a disappointment. Between 1991 and 1993 he made 22 appearances (seven more as a substitute) and scored three goals before being sold to Sheffield United. He was a player of undoubted talent who seemed to lack self-belief; far too often he would hide in a game.

CARR, JACK. This solid defender who played between 1899 and 1912 was a rugged, dependable left-back who signed from Seaton Burn. Carr went on to represent his country (England) and was, by all accounts, a genuinely nice man. He made 277 appearances for the Magpies and scored five goals.

CARR, KEVIN. Ashington-born goalkeeper who looked set for an outstanding career in the Newcastle goal, Carr made 195 appearances for the club before moving to Carlisle. He fell foul of some desperate luck. First, whilst at Newcastle, he walked through a glass partitioning door; then, at Carlisle, he was involved in a car crash. Thankfully, he was not seriously hurt, though his goalkeeping confidence appeared to shatter with the glass door. He was never the same keeper. He made just 17 appearances for Carlisle, which included some of the worst performances in his career. Despite his poor luck, Kevin Carr cared deeply for the fans, especially those of Newcastle United.

CARTWRIGHT, PETER. Midfielder who signed from North Shields in June 1979. Cartwright made 58 appearances (11 more as a substitute) and scored four times for the club before being sold to Darlington in March 1983.

CARVER, JESSE. Signed from Blackburn Rovers for a £2,000 fee. Carver made 76 appearances without a goal between 1936 and 1939. He later progressed into management and saw successful seasons abroad with Juventus and Torino.

CASEY, THOMAS. An Irish-born wing-half who signed from Bournemouth in August 1952, Casey went on to represent his country (Northern Ireland) on ten occasions whilst at St James's. He made 132 Newcastle appearances and scored ten goals. Casey was sold to Portsmouth in July 1958, and later moved into club management with several League and non-League outfits.

CASSIDY, THOMAS. Outstanding midfeld player who signed from Irish side Coleraine in October 1970. Cassidy was a workhorse in the United midfield. An Irish international, he was a born leader, a man who would never let his head drop no matter how badly things were going. He scored 26 goals in his 212 appearances (and played 13 more games as a substitute). Cassidy's role in the United side between 1970 and 1980 should never be under-estimated. He moved to Burnley in July 1980 but his roots on Tyneside were never broken. He recently managed Gateshead in the GM Vauxhall Conference. In manage-ment, he is as ambitious as he was as a player.

CHALMERS, WILLIAM. Chalmers was signed from Glasgow Rangers as a goalscorer with a big reputation. He remained at the club between 1928 and 1931, making 42 appearances and scoring 13 goals. A real character, Chalmers would often indulge in friendly banter with the crowd.

CHANDLER, ALBERT. A full-back brought in for a £3,250 fee from Derby County, Chandler never settled at the club but made 36 appearances in his solitary season, 1925–26.

CHANNON, MICK. In 1982 the Newcastle management were desperately seeking out an elusive idol who would motivate and enthuse their loyal fans. Mick Channon, however, was not the player to fill this role. Seen as the ideal strike partner for Kevin Keegan, Channon failed to inspire, and made just four appearances, scoring once, during his brief sojourn to the North East. He moved to Bristol Rovers later that same year.

CHARLTON, JACK. Jack Charlton was Newcastle's team manager between June 1984 and August 1985. As a player, Charlton had had a tremendous career – indeed as a manager he has been nothing but successful; his time at United, though, was a torrid one. Charlton was, by his very nature, relaxed in his attitude. On his arrival at Newcastle, the press wrote: 'One of the North East's favourite sons has returned to his rightful home.' Everything went well – until Big Jack began his fishing trips. Fans and officials did not take kindly to their manager being away from the club during the week in order to indulge in his favourite hobby: fishing. His first season in charge saw the club finish 14th in the First Division. At the beginning of season 1985–86 Charlton was barracked by the crowd who were unhappy about some of the signings he had made. Without further ado he walked out of the club and vowed never to return to club management; a sad end to a marvellous club career. His international managerial duties since then have proved his outstanding ability in this field, however.

CLARK, FRANK. What can one say about this outstanding defender? Clark was signed from a non-League side, Crook Town, turning professional in November 1962. The tall, well-built full-back was one of the best of his time. No one in Tyneside who saw him in action could understand why he was overlooked for a full international call-up. Between 1962 and 1975 he made a Newcastle career total of 456 appearances (one more as a substitute), and scored just once! Clark comes across as a dour man but is in fact extremely pleasant and one of the most genuine footballers ever to grace St James's Park or don the black-and-white shirt.

In July 1975 he moved to Nottingham Forest where he made well over a hundred appearances and won even more honours. Later he moved into management with Sunderland, Notts Forest and then Orient, where he became managing director. He returned to Forest as manager, where he has built an outstanding club side with much promise for the future.

CLARK, LEE. Local lad turned hero, Lee Clark is an outstanding prospect for the future. Already he has achieved U-21 international recognition and has worked hard to break into the United first team despite the presence of the big-name stars already holding down his midfield/attacking role. Clark will, I am certain, become a United regular and crowd favourite. Even his often petulant nature has been harnessed by his manager and used to the player's own advantage. Born in Wallsend there was only ever one club for him.

CLARK, ROBERT. Striker who played between 1923 and 1928 and scored 16 goals from 77 first-team appearances. Clark was one of several frontmen employed by the club for a short period of time.

CLARKE, JEFF. A Yorkshire-born defender who signed from Sunderland in August 1982, Clarke made 134 appearances for Newcastle, scoring five goals, his second-best career total. (His best was 178 appearances and six goals for Sunderland.) The strong centre-half could have greatly improved his United record had he not picked up an injury. Played overseas for Ankara in 1987 but returned to Tyneside and took up a role as 'Football in the Community' officer before his promotion to reserve-team coach in 1993.

CLARKE, RAY. Ray Clarke was a former England youth international when he arrived at Newcastle from Brighton

Lee Clark

and Hove Albion in July 1980. Clarke had also played overseas for FC Bruges. A Londoner by birth, he found life in the North uncomfortable. In 1980–81, his sole playing season at the club, he made 18 appearances and scored three goals.

CLIFTON, HENRY. An £8,500 signing from Chesterfield in 1938, Clifton was a talented inside-left whose career at United was badly disrupted by the outbreak of war. In all, he made 35 appearances for the club and netted 17 goals. There were also some 42 Wartime League appearances which resulted in 27 goals. After the war he moved to Grimsby Town.

CLISH, COLIN. After escalating through the ranks to take up the position of full-back for 20 games, Clish was unfortunate to be surrounded by quality defenders who overtook him in his ambition for first-team football. He was later transferred to Rotherham United in December 1963, moving on to Doncaster in 1968.

COLE, ANDY. The outstanding goalscorer and United frontman Andy Cole arrived from Bristol City having started his professional career first at Arsenal, which included a brief loan spell with Fulham. Any player who can near United's all-time season's best of 36 goals by an individual has to be something special. Cole grabbed himself 34 goals in the 1993–94 campaign, just two short of Hughie Gallacher's record. Put simply, Cole's pace, turn and shooting prowess are second to none. Pundits and fans alike hailed him as the greatest striker England had ever known. He was the terrace idol of the '90s.

Then the unbelievable happened. Cole went nine matches without scoring in the 1994–95 campaign. There were signs of unrest as the media speculated as to his quality of life on Tyneside. Then came the devastating news no Newcastle fan wanted to hear: Cole has been sold to Manchester United. The golden boy of the terraces was gone. The media attempted to whip up a frenzy in the city, but failed miserably. Of course there were one or two who called for Keegan's head, but the majority supported their manager's decisions – Manchester United had, after all, paid £7 million for the player *and* given Newcastle the talented youngster, Keith Gillespie. Despite this, Andy Cole produced many glorious moments for Newcastle United fans to savour. Whether his career will prosper elsewhere is open to debate.

COLLINS, JAMES. Striker who played for the club in two separate spells, in 1892–93 and then 1895–97. During the latter period he was more successful, bagging 11 goals in 42

Andy Cole

appearances. One of several strikers tried by the club in the early part of its history.

COLOURS. Ask any United supporter and they will assure you that Newcastle have always played in black and white! In fact, the club's first strip consisted of red shirts with white shorts. It was not until 2 August 1894 that the famous black-and-white stripes were introduced. (*Note*: the stripes have to be two inches wide!)

45

CONNELL, J. Another forward tried in the club's early days. Connell made 25 appearances and scored three goals for the club in the season of 1896–97.

CONNELLY, EDWARD. Inside-forward signed from Scottish club side Dumbarton, who was just 19 years of age when he made his United debut. In his three-year spell with the club he made 30 appearances and scored nine goals. After the war he played for Luton Town, Orient and Brighton and Hove Albion.

CONNOLLY, JOHN. Midfielder who came to Newcastle in May 1978 via Everton and Birmingham City. This Scottish international played a beautiful pass, and possessed a unique eye for a goal. Some of his efforts were more than a bit special, from top-corner goals to bending the ball around defenders. Connolly made 43 appearances (eight more as a substitute) and scored ten goals for the club.

COOPER, EDWARD. Right-winger signed for a fee of £1,300 from Glossop in 1913. Cooper had a terrific burst of speed which caught out the opposition. All too often he failed to deliver the goods though, with his fellow forwards left frustrated by his poor crossing. Between 1913 and 1920 he played 46 times for the club and scored twice. In a further ten appearances during the war he scored two more goals.

COOPER, JOSEPH. Half-back signed from Winlaton Mill in September 1952. Cooper was a strong player who persevered and won his personal battles on the field. He made just six appearances between 1953 and 1957, and enjoyed his football with the club. A good professional.

COPELAND, EDWARD. Local-born outside-right who made 20 wartime appearances for the club, scoring three goals. Copeland went on to play a solitary season with Hartlepool United in 1946–47 after active service.

CORBETT, ROBERT. Another local product signed from Throckley Welfare just after the war, Corbett was a no-

nonsense full-back who took no prisoners, making each tackle as though his very life depended upon it. He made 60 appearances and scored two goals between 1943 and 1951. Further appearances were made during the war, giving him a total of 62.

CORNER-KICKS. In what must be a unique record, United faced Portsmouth in a League Division 1 fixture at St James's Park on Saturday, 5th December 1931. The final score was 0–0. Throughout the game not a solitary corner-kick was awarded to either side! Negative attack, or good defending? Thank goodness I missed that one!

CORNWELL, JOHN. London-born midfielder who came to the club in 1987 from Orient. Cornwell found the going a little tough in the Newcastle first team, and his footballing days were limited to just 32 appearances and one goal. A player who never settled, Cornwell returned south to Swindon Town in the 1988–89 season.

COSMOPOLITAN. Today the local council would like to claim that the city of Newcastle is cosmopolitan and certainly the United line-up for the 1952 FA Cup final was. It boasted four Englishmen, three Scots, two Chileans, an Irishman, and a Welshman. Today's 'three foreigners' regulation would have left the United team decimated.

COWAN, JOHN. Northern Ireland international inside-forward who came to St James's Park from Irish side Crusaders. Cowan found it difficult to break into the first team and made just six appearances with a further four as a substitute during a six-year spell between 1967 and 1973. He later played for Darlington.

COWAN, WILLIAM. Inside-forward who signed for a fee of £2,250 from Dundee. Cowan played for Scotland whilst with the club. A good quality, attacking player with a big heart; several United stars of the era remember him as outstanding in his contribution to each and every game. Between 1923 and 1926 he made 101 appearances and scored 28 goals.

John Cornwell

COWELL, ROBERT. Bobby Cowell was signed from Blackhall Colliery Welfare shortly after the end of the Second World War. As a full-back, the man was a colossus amongst his peers. He was a thorough professional whose love for the club was evident in his performances. Dedication and devotion saw him make no less than 327 appearances between 1946 and 1954, throughout which time he managed to avoid serious injury. Cowell always erred on the side of safety, rather than risk anything reckless. He was totally dependable, the kind of player who would fit into today's football world without any problem. He also managed some 81 Wartime League appearances!

COX, ARTHUR. United manager between September 1980 and May 1984. Cox came to the club when it languished in Division 2. In 1982 he pulled off one of the biggest coups ever achieved by the club, namely the signing of Kevin Keegan. He followed this up with Terry McDermott and, a short while later, one Peter Beardsley. Meanwhile, youngsters like Chris Waddle were making names for themselves. Cox created a side worthy of competing with the best. In 1983–84 United were promoted back into Division I but in the summer of that same year Cox walked out of the club after contractual disagreements. From there he managed Derby County before returning to Newcastle in the summer of 1994, this time as Keegan's assistant. Cox has a good track-record as a manager, is well respected in the game and his experience can only enhance United's style.

CRAGGS, JOHN. The thick-set full-back John Craggs was rock-solid in the United defence. Born in Flint Hill, he burst through the club's junior ranks and into the first team, signing professional in December 1965. Craggs in fact had two spells at the club. The first between 1966 and 1970, saw him gain several honours including youth international recognition. He made 50 appearances for United and scored once. He made a further two appearances as a substitute. He then moved to Middlesbrough in 1971, before returning to St James's Park in August 1982 when he went on to make a further 18 appearances, with three more as a substitute, and score once more for the club. As his name suggests, Craggs was a rugged player who enjoyed his football, especially so in the North East. He later moved to Darlington in August 1983.

CRAIG, ALBERT. Striker who failed to score in seven full matches for the club. A further five substitute appearances were little better as Craig suffered a loss of form. He arrived from Hamilton Academical and was actually loaned back to them during his brief stay at Newcastle. Eventually, though, he moved to Northampton Town where his record was a formidable two appearances, one goal.

CRAIG, BEN. As a full-back who came to the club in 1938 and remained with them until after the war, 1950 to be precise, Craig made 67 appearances for the club without scoring. He had been spotted when playing for Huddersfield Town. He maintained ties with United for some 44 years, until his death in 1982.

CRAIG, DAVID. 25 Northern Ireland caps, one U-23 cap and an Irish youth international; we are talking class here. Defender David Craig remained with Newcastle between 1962 and 1978. His totals – 16 years, 406 appearances (plus six as a substitute) and 12 goals – are a formidable record. Reliable, a born leader, devoted, sensible, Craig was all of these and more. Arriving at Newcastle as a youngster, David was a man with a mission, to play for the first team, which he achieved. He appeared in several finals wearing United colours, and always held his head high with pride. Probably the best defensive player United have ever had, David Craig was, quite simply, Newcastle United.

CRAIG, THOMAS. Another Scottish international midfielder was Tommy Craig. The short, well-built player with the distinctive fair hair had come to Tyneside from Sheffield Wednesday, where he had enjoyed a marvellous career, making 210 appearances for the Owls. United prised him away from Hillsborough in December 1974 and he remained at St James's Park until January 1978. Craig had a pair of magical feet, capable of accurate passing and phenomenal shooting. He was as complete a midfield player as United ever had. In all, he turned out 150 times, twice more as a substitute, and scored 29 goals. He later signed for Aston Villa, Swansea and finally Carlisle, where he reproduced some of his best form. One memorable goal was a precise lob from 30 yards against a resurgent Sheffield Wednesday. Two more against United were so finely placed

Tommy Craig

that only the educated boot of Craig could have planted them there.

CRATE, THOMAS. Joined Newcastle East End from local football in 1891 and progressed to make the first team of the newly formed Newcastle United in their inaugural League fixture at Royal Arsenal on 2 September 1893. Crate was a bustling centre-forward and has the distinction of scoring United's first-ever League goal in the 2–2 draw. He stayed with United until 1895, made a total of 41 appearances and scored 15 goals. His first goal earns him a special place in United's history.

CRIELLY, ROBERT. Another Newcastle East End star who remained with the club until it became United. Bob Crielly was a midfield player and usually wore the number-4 shirt. He played in United's first-ever League game, made 59 appearances and scored one goal for United. Crielly was noted as being a little hot-headed and found himself in trouble several times with club officials. Nonetheless, he was a player of some distinction in those early days.

CROPLEY, ALEX. Scottish international midfielder whose father was a professional with Aldershot. Cropley's career began at Hibernian before he moved to England with Arsenal and then Aston Villa. His move to Newcastle was but a temporary loan spell and he never quite made his presence felt. He made just three appearances in 1980 before returning to Villa Park.

CROSSON, DAVID. Durham-born defender who rose through the club's junior set-up. Crosson signed professional terms for United in November 1970 and made all of his six first-team appearances in the 1973–74 season. Despite this, he remained in the reserves until his move to Darlington in August 1975, where he went on to make 115 appearances.

CROWE, CHARLES. Byker-born wing-half Crowe was a real gem. Picked up from Wallsend St Leonards, he joined United in 1944. Solid in the tackle, quick in the turn, and formidable when running forward, Crowe made 192 appearances for the club and scored five goals between 1944 and 1957. He also featured in 24 Wartime League games, scoring a further goal. Fans on the terraces, with typical Geordie wit, would cry out: 'Give the ball to Crowe and let him fly!' Crowe certainly could.

CROWN, LAURIE. Defender signed from South Shields in 1926 who spent just one season at St James's Park, when he turned out twice for the club, without scoring.

CUMMINGS, ROBERT. Ashington-born Cummings joined the club from North Hartley in May 1954. As a forward he had been prolific in front of goal in the local leagues. His first spell at the club between 1954 and 1956 saw him as a squad player. He was transferred to Aberdeen before coming home in October 1963 and, between 1963 and 1965, he made 43 appearances, one more as a substitute, and scored 14 goals. He was transferred to Darlington in October 1965.

CUNNINGHAM, ANDY. Andy Cunningham was one of Scotland's all-time great footballers. Having played almost 450 games for Rangers and won just about every honour the Scottish game could offer (including seven Championship medals), this very talented inside-right signed for Newcastle in February 1929 for £2,300. By this time he was 38 years old (he holds the record as United's oldest debutant!). After 15 games and two goals for Newcastle he retired from playing in May 1930. In January of that year he had actually become the club's first-ever manager, guiding United to FA Cup glory in 1932. The euphoria of victory was short-lived, however, as the club suffered relegation to Division 2 a couple of years later. Poor form and a declining position in the League led to Cunningham's resignation as manager at the end of season 1934–35.

Andy Cunningham sadly died in May 1973. His wealth of experience was certainly put to good use by Newcastle United.

CURRY, TOM. The adpatable Tom Curry was originally brought in as a wing-half but was tested in a number of positions as injuries and wartime service decimated the professional game. Despite such setbacks, Curry made 235 appearances and scored five goals. He later went on to coach the great Manchester United side of the 1950s. He was one of those killed in the tragic Munich Air disaster of 1958.

CURRY, WILLIAM. Newcastle-born centre-forward who joined the Magpies in October 1953. He played 88 times, scoring 40 goals, until his departure to Brighton and Hove Albion in July 1959.

D

DALTON, GEORGE. A full-back who was born and bred in Newcastle, Dalton progressed through the United juniors before breaking into the first team in 1960. He went on to play 94 games and score two goals.

DAVIDSON, DAVID. Signed from Liverpool in 1930, Davidson was a strong and determined full-back who made 144 appearances for the club between 1930 and 1937.

DAVIDSON, TOM. Davidson arrived from Millwall Athletic in 1901 as a full-back. Made 43 appearances. Remained with the club until 1903.

DAVIES, ALAN. Davies made his name with Manchester United when he played his debut match – the FA Cup final. He came to St James's Park in 1985 with high hopes of proving himself to be a quality winger. Injuries and lack of self-belief did little to make this a reality, though. Davies left United in 1987 with 22 appearances (two more as a substitute) and a single goal to his credit. A relative youngster, he sadly died in 1992 whilst on Swansea City's books.

DAVIES, IAN. A defender who made 81 appearances between 1979 and 1982, scoring four goals, Davies moved to Manchester City in August 1982.

DAVIES, REG. This Welsh international who won six full caps was an inside-forward. He joined United in April 1951, played 170 games and scored 50 goals, before transferring to Swansea City in October 1958.

DAVIES, WYN. One of United's all-time great strikers, the tall, lean Davies possessed a bullet header and fine ball-skills. He was a terrific goalscorer whose success ensured a long, outstanding career at nine League clubs: Wrexham, Bolton, Manchester City, Manchester United, Blackpool, Crystal Palace, Stockport, Crewe and Newcastle. He was at Newcastle between 1966 and 1971. Originally signed from Bolton, Davies made no less than 216 appearances and scored 53 goals, ten of which were in European competitions. As a Welsh international he was capped 11 times whilst at Newcastle. He moved to Manchester City in August 1971.

DAY, WILLIAM. An outside-right who never really made it at the club, Day was signed from Middlesbrough in March 1962. He made 14 appearances, scoring once, before moving to Peterborough in April 1963.

DEBUTS. Billy Foulkes signed for United in 1951, just ten days before he made his international debut for Wales in a game against England. His first kick of the ball was extremely successful – he scored! A rather unique debut for a United player.

Meanwhile, Thomas Pearson, who was 34 years and 27 days old when he made his international debut for Scotland, is the second-oldest debutant in the history of the Scottish international game. Curiously, due to a loss of form, he was dropped by United around the same time!

DEFEATS. United's worst-ever defeat was a 9–0 beating in a Division 2 fixture at Burton Wanderers on 15 April 1895.

The worst-ever home defeat is more embarrassing. Sunderland came to St James's Park on 5 December 1908 and, with an incredible eight-goal burst in the last 28 minutes, beat the home side 9–1!

The longest United have gone without defeat stands at 17 games, between April and October 1992.

The longest United have gone without defeat at home stands at 24 games, between October 1968 and August 1969.

The longest United have gone without defeat away stands at 11 games, between November 1907 and March 1908.

DENMARK, JIMMY. At 6'1" tall and of slim build, Jimmy Denmark was a dominant centre-half and a great header of the ball. Formerly with Third Lanark, he made 51 appearances for United between 1937 and 1946.

DENNISON, ROBERT. Dennison was a Cumbrian-born centre-half who made 11 appearances and scored two goals for the club between 1929 and 1934. He later moved to Nottingham Forest, Fulham and Northampton Town, He also had a career in club management at the Cobblers, Middlesbrough and Hereford United.

DEVINE, JOSEPH. Signed from Burnley for the huge fee of £5,575 in 1930. He was the forward who scored in the 1–0 victory over West Ham on the last day of the 1929–30 season, thus keeping United in first-division football for a further season. Made 22 appearances and scored 11 goals in one year at the club.

DICKSON, C. Forward who arrived from Dundee in 1894 and who made 23 outings for the first team, scoring 12 goals, during 1894–95.

DILLON, KEVIN. Sunderland-born midfielder who had won himself a great reputation at Birmingham and Portsmouth, Dillon signed for Newcastle in 1989 but was hardly inspiring. He found the going tough when better quality players began arriving at the club. His enthusiasm ensured he would give his all in a game but this was not always sufficient. He made 71 appearances and one as a substitute between 1989 and 1991. He was transferred to Bournemouth and now plays non-League soccer.

DINNIS, RICHARD. Richard Dinnis managed United through one of the club's most turbulent periods. Originally on Blackburn Rovers' books, Dinnis never made a professional appearance as a footballer. He joined the Rovers coaching staff under Gordon Lee and, when the latter moved to Newcastle as manager, Dinnis went with him. When Lee later left United the players were in uproar and threatened to go on strike. Dinnis, meanwhile, was made team manager and was able to quell the problem as United progressed into Europe – only to lose to Bastia. On the domestic front, United were bottom of Division 1 and Dinnis was duly sacked after managing the club from February to November 1977.

DIXON, STANLEY. A forward who signed from local non-League side Barrington Albion, Dixon remained at United between 1914 and 1923. He spent much of his time in the reserves but managed 53 appearances and ten goals for the first team. He also made eight Wartime League appearances for the club.

DOCKING, S. Reserve striker who made 21 outings and scored three goals between 1934 and 1938.

DODGIN, NORMAN. Wing-half who came to the club in 1940 and stayed for a decade. Dodgin made 86 appearances and scored once before moving to Reading in June 1950. United originally signed him from Whitehall Boys Club.

DONALDSON, ANDREW. Signed from Vickers Armstrong in 1943, this solidly-built centre-forward made 19 senior outings and netted six goals. Donaldson was transferred to Middlesbrough in January 1949, and later went on to Exeter City.

DOUGLAS, ANGUS. Scottish international forward who came via Chelsea for a fee of £1,100 in 1913. His goalscoring prowess was not as evident on Tyneside, with only two goals coming from 56 games.

DUFFY, ALAN. England youth international forward who signed professional in March 1967. Made only two first-team appearances (plus two more as a substitute) before moving to Brighton in January 1970.

DUFFY, CHRISTOPHER. Very much a stand-in forward between 1906 and 1908, Duffy had arrived via Middlesbrough and made 16 appearances with one goal to his credit.

DUNCAN, JOHN. John Duncan was an honest, hard-working forward whose arrival on Tyneside was a huge leap from the rural surroundings of Ayr United's Somerset Park, from whom he was signed in 1950. Duncan made five appearances for Newcastle and scored three goals in a three-year spell with the club.

DUNCAN, SCOTT. Appeared in United colours between 1908 and 1913 and made 81 appearances, scoring 11 times. Duncan was a youngster whose solid performances in the United line-up brought him great admiration from the St James's crowd.

DYSON, KEITH. This forward was a product of United's brilliant youth scheme of the 1960s. Dyson signed professional in August 1968. He attracted the attention of the likes of Shankly of Liverpool and Revie of Leeds, both of whom spoke of him as being the most outstanding young player of his time. Despite their efforts, neither could part him from St James's Park.

Dyson made a total of 92 appearances for United, four more as a substitute, and scored 26 goals – including a European match-winner against Dundee United in the 1969–70 Fairs Cup, first round, second leg. A further European goal was notched up against Anderlecht that same season.

Dyson had exquisite ball control, balance and tenacity. He may well have felt that all the attention upon his undoubted skill weighed too heavily upon him because, rather than progress, he seemed to stagnate. Eventually he was used as part of a transfer deal which took him to Blackpool and brought the exciting little forward Tony Green to St James's Park in October 1971.

E

EAST STAND. Standing proudly opposite the players' tunnel bearing the club name on its roofing fascia, the East Stand was one of the first parts of the old St James's Park to be modernised. It sits in front of the huge St James's Hospital.

EASTHAM, GEORGE. The Blackpool-born soccer legend George Eastham was the son of a professional footballer also named George. Eastham junior signed for United in May 1956 at only 20 years of age. Eastham was strong, rugged and agile, a typical 1950s centre-forward prepared to challenge for any ball that entered the penalty area even if there was little hope of catching it.

He went on to make a total of 129 appearances for the Magpies and scored 34 goals. However, his latter stages at the club are memorable for his desire to leave. It is natural for any footballer to want to better himself and Eastham saw a move to Arsenal as the ideal opportunity to further his career. The Newcastle manager, Charlie Mitten, refused to let him go though, with any future transfer request from the player being automatically denied. Eastham remonstrated with the club, but to no avail. He sought legal advice and, eventually, with a wealthy sponsor behind him, he went on strike. He got his wish and was transferred to Arsenal in November 1960. A subsequent high-court hearing between Eastham and United saw the Judge support Eastham's claim that as a footballer he had as much right as any working person to choose his employer. Thus players could negotiate for new contracts once old ones had expired.

EDGAR, EDWARD. Bristol-born goalkeeper who made it through the United juniors before signing professional in August 1978. Edgar made just one appearance between the sticks in his three-year spell as a professional between 1973 and 1976. He transferred to Hartlepool United in July 1976, where he made over 75 appearances.

ELLIOTT, DAVID. Midfielder who signed from Sunderland in the December of 1966 and went on to star in several memorable United performances, in particular those in European competition against Feyenoord and Sporting Lisbon. Elliott was a dynamo, a hundred-mile-an-hour player with amazing stamina. He made 86 appearances for the club, four more as a substitute, and scored four goals. He moved to Southend United in February 1971.

ELLIOTT, ROBBIE. Gosforth-born Robbie Elliott made his name in the United first team when injuries forced Keegan to introduce him. To everyone's surprise the youngster performed with alarming maturity befitting one of much greater experience. Something of a utility player, Elliott will no doubt have a good football career ahead of him.

ELLISON, RAYMOND. Ray Ellison joined his home-town club as an apprentice and signed professional in October 1968. He made six appearances as a full-back during a five-year spell with the club. He transferred to Sunderland in March 1973.

ELLISON, ROY. Roy Ellison is distinguished for a rather indifferent United career as he never actually made a first-team appearance for the club. Signed as an apprentice and a

Robbie Elliott

forward, he turned professional in June 1966 but soon found himself surplus to requirements. He transferred to Barrow in February 1968 where he scored nine goals in 78 games. He later moved to Hartlepool United.

END, GALLOWGATE. St James's Park is more commonly referred to by locals as Gallowgate. The Gallowgate End was once the open terrace of the ground, which was partly

63

used by away support. I can recall its grand old scoreboard of the 1960s which seemed to dominate the ground. Sadly, the Gallowgate is no more. It is now an all-seater ultra-modern stand. To the uninitiated, the Gallowgate is the end which sits immediately to the right of the East Stand as you look from the club's main entrance. It stands in Gallowgate, a main route through the city.

END, LEAZES. The Leazes End is part of Newcastle United folklore. It is the spion kop of the ground where millions have stood in adulation over the years worshipping their gods upon the pitch. The Leazes End, or Leazes Park End was covered in 1930 until 1978 when the roof was taken down and United were relegated to Division 2! From there on in the Leazes End was never the same. It was drastically reduced in size in order that foundations for the East Stand could be built. Today it is gloriously all-seated, more palatial and more pleasing to the eye. The Leazes End will never be quite the same, but today's supporters are as fanatical as ever and create a terrific atmosphere all their own.

EVANS, REGINALD. Consett-born forward who signed professional in March 1956, Evans appeared capable enough in front of goal but found it difficult to break into the first team. Between 1956 and 1959 he made just four appearances, without a goal to his credit. He transferred to Charlton Athletic in March 1959, where he scored twice in 14 games.

EVANS, THOMAS. United's first-ever Welsh international, Evans was a full-back who cost £3,650 when he was bought from Clapton Orient in 1927. He remained on Tyneside between 1927 and 1930 but was continually on the treatment table with injury after injury. His career total is 13 appearances for Newcastle, with one goal.

F

FA CUP. United have appeared in no less than 11 FA Cup finals. They won in 1910, 1924, 1932, 1951, 1952 and 1955, and were losing finalists in 1905, 1906, 1908, 1911 and 1974. They have appeared in the competition's semi-finals on 13 occasions.

FA YOUTH CUP. United have won this competition twice, in 1962 and 1985.

FAIRBROTHER, JACK. This outstanding goalkeeper, who hailed from Burton, began his professional career at Preston North End, where he made 41 appearances before signing for Newcastle in July 1947. The ex-policeman made a total of 144 first-team appearances for the Magpies, before going on to manage Gateshead. Renowned for his dogged professionalism, he would work out his positioning by using lengths of string to show the goalpost angles!

FAIRHURST, DAVID. Full-back who was signed from Midlands side, Walsall. Fairhurst was a consistent performer and proved himself a worthy signing with 284 appearances and two goals between 1929 and 1946.

FAIRS CUP, INTER CITIES. United have entered this competition three times and won it once; in 1969 when they beat Ujpest Dozsa 6–2 on aggregate. The United team and scorers were: (first leg) (h) McFaul, Craig, Clark, Gibb, Burton, Moncur (2), Scott (1), Robson, Davies, Arentoft and Sinclair (3–0 victory). For the second leg (a), United fielded precisely the same team, and won 3–2, the scorers being Moncur, Arentoft and Foggon, who came on as a substitute.

FASHANU, JUSTIN. Renowned for a spectacular goal which he scored for Norwich City, Justin Fashanu failed to live up to expectations. He came to Tyneside as an experiment more than anything else. It was a chance for him to prove himself again, but he made only one appearance, as a substitute, in 1991.

FELL, JAMES. A speedy left-winger, Fell had a terrific turn of pace. Signed from Everton in March 1962, he went on to make 53 appearances and score 17 goals in 1962–63. He was transferred to Walsall in July 1963.

FERDINAND, LES. The arrival of Les Ferdinand on Tyneside came as a surprise to everyone except fans of Newcastle United. For much of season 1994–95 rumours were rife that Ferdinand wanted to join the Magpies, and his wish has now been granted. The former QPR striker will add a new dimension to the United attack as the tough, no-nonsense centre-forward has the panache and creativity to make goals out of nothing. His career began with Hayes before a move to QPR in 1986. Loan spells followed, first at Brentford in 1987–88 and then at Besiktas in 1988–89. By 1990, however, the potential which had attracted Rangers in the first place began to shine through. His outstanding aerial abilities came to the fore and goals quickly followed. A full England international, Les Ferdinand is destined to become another number 9 hero at St James's Park.

FEREDAY, WAYNE. This midfielder from Queens Park Rangers arrived at Newcastle in 1989. He never really fitted in with his new environment and was transferred to

Bournemouth after just 31 appearances, with seven more as a substitute.

FERGUSON, BRIAN. Another midfielder who flattered to deceive, Ferguson was an ex-Mansfield Town apprentice and showed plenty of promise in his early years. He signed for United in January 1979, made four appearances (one more as a substitute) and scored once before moving to Hull City in December 1980.

FERGUSON, ROBERT. Born in Dudley, Robert Ferguson progressed through the United juniors before signing professional in May 1955. As a full-back he made 11 appearances for the club before returning to the Midlands and Derby County in October 1962.

FINES. Prior to the 1924 FA Cup final against Villa, United fielded a weakened side for a fixture against their Cup final opponents. Villa won the League fixture 6–1 and Newcastle won the FA Cup 2–0. However, in view of the weakened side fielded for the League fixture, the Football Association fined United £750. Curiously, United were fined £50 before the 1906 final and £100 prior to the 1901 final for precisely the same breach of FA rules!

FINLAY, JOCK. Signed from Airdrie for a fee of £775, Jock Finlay proved to be one of the best signings United ever made. He was a left-half whose pinpoint passing and swivel upon the ball was a pleasure to watch. Finlay made his United debut aged just 16 and went on to make 161 appearances, scoring eight goals between 1909 and 1927.

FLOODLIGHTS. The first-ever floodlit game between League sides took place at St James's Park, between Carlisle United and Darlington in an FA Cup replay on Monday, 28 November 1955. United's floodlights were installed in February 1953. Incidentally, United also featured in the first League fixture played under lights, which was Portsmouth v Newcastle on Wednesday 22 February 1956. United won 2–0.

FOG. Never has fog played such an important part in United's history as it did on 26 November 1904. Everton, who were challenging for the Championship along with United, were playing an away fixture at Woolwich Arsenal. Everton were 3–1 up with 12 minutes to go when fog caused the match to be abandoned. The Woolwich v Everton game had to be replayed; this time, though. Woolwich won 2–1. The loss of the points ensured that Newcastle were champions. Had the previous result stood as an Everton win, then *they* would have been champions!

FOGGON, ALAN. Foggon was a tall, well-built forward from Chester-le-Street, Durham. His great frame carried immense power and the player had a thunderous shot and header to match. He was a United apprentice who signed professional in November 1967. He went on to make a total of 69 appearances for the club, 11 more as a substitute, and scored 16 goals. Foggon was eventually sold to Cardiff City in August 1971, before returning to England to star for Middlesbrough.

FORD, DAVID. Slim-built, inside-forward who signed from Sheffield Wednesday in December 1969. Ford arrived at Newcastle aiming to prove himself a big hit with the fans. Injuries and inconsistent form saw him make just 28 appearances, though (three more as a substitute), and score three goals between 1969 and 1971. Nobody was more disappointed than Ford that he never quite made it on Tyneside. He returned to Sheffield, this time to Bramall Lane.

FOULKES, WILLIAM. Welsh international forward signed from Chester City in May 1958. Billy Foulkes was a no-nonsense player who was tough, shrewd and capable. He knew where the goal was and was never afraid to shoot. His instinct as to the positioning of others around him was incredible. Time and again he would lay off the perfect pass or cross. Between 1951 and 1954 he made a total of 68 appearances for the club and scored nine goals. He moved to Southampton in August 1954.

FOUNDED. Newcastle United was created from Newcastle East End, who had been one of two local club sides, the other being Newcastle West End, who were swallowed up by their neighbours. West End had always played at St James's Park so the ground lease was handed over to East End when they amalgamated. East End had been formed in 1882. On 9 December 1892, after public meetings, Newcastle East End formally became known as Newcastle United and became a limited company on 6 September 1895.

FOX, RUEL. Signed from Norwich City, Ruel Fox, although a diminutive character, plays like a giant. With an amazing turn of speed he has the commitment to make himself a real terrace idol. Although he occasionally lets his head drop when things are going against him, a great deal more responsibility has been placed on him after the departure of his striking partner, Andy Cole.

FOYERS, ROBERT. Scottish international left-back who signed from Edinburgh St Bernard's in 1895 for a fee of £100. Today Foyers would probably cost in excess of £500,000, which shows how highly he was thought of last century. Made 39 appearances for the club.

FRANKS, ALBERT. Midfield dynamo signed from Boldon Colliery Welfare in December 1953. Franks was as dependable a player as one could have hoped for. He made 75 appearances and scored four goals between 1953 and 1960. He later signed for Glasgow Rangers who had recognised his potential early on.

FRASER, JACK. Enthusiastic winger who joined the club from Notts County in 1899. Fraser was the archetypal left-winger: lean and dangerous when on the move with the ball at his feet. He made 52 appearances and scored nine goals between 1899 and 1901.

FRASER, RONNIE. Giant centre-half who was signed from Hibernian after the war. Made 27 outings for the first team during his four years on Tyneside between 1946 and 1950.

He was 30 years old when he joined United, so was already in the latter stages of his career.

Ruel Fox

G

GALLACHER, HUGH. Diminutive striker who was often described as an 'absolute genius'. Wee Hughie Gallacher came to Newcastle in 1925 as a raw 22-year-old. He had previously played all his football in Scotland, Queen of the South and Airdrie being the best known of his Scottish associations.

Hughie was a prolific goalscorer. On his United debut on 12 December 1925, v Everton, the 36,000 crowd were amazed by his electrifying scoring prowess when he netted twice. The game ended in a 3–3 draw, with another outstanding striker of the era, Dixie Deans, scoring a hat-trick for Everton! There was a buzz of anticipation every time Gallacher got the ball. He was a real crowd-pleaser and he played up to his audience. And why not? A player who could create such enthusiastic reaction from the watching hordes has a right to do his own thing.

Gallacher was made team captain and with his fiery temper was a real motivator. His short, stocky frame whizzed around the pitch, willing himself on until he won possession. This Scottish international went on to make 174 appearances for the club, and scored a fantastic 143 goals, including 36 in one record-breaking season.

Much to everyone's sadness, including his own, he was sold to Chelsea for a huge £10,000 fee in 1930. Gallacher did not wish to leave, and the whole of the city of Newcastle was in uproar when his move was announced. Hughie returned with his new club and created an all-time attendance record at St James's Park of 68,586. It was claimed that a further 40,000 were locked out as Newcastle United supporters came to pay homage to their ex-idol. United won the fixture 1–0, with Jackie Cape stealing the headlines with a 76th-minute headed winner.

In 1934 Gallacher moved to Derby County. By now he was bankrupt and on a downward spiral. He later moved to Notts County and then Grimsby Town before a brief spell with Gateshead. Always one to speak his mind, Gallacher moved into local sports journalism and was actually banned from St James's Park for severely criticising the Newcastle side and management.

In 1957, after a dreadful period of personal grief, Wee Hughie threw himself in front of the York–Edinburgh express train at Dead Man's Crossing, Low Fell. It was an ignominious end for a man who had brought so much pleasure to so many people.

GALLACHER, JOHN. Striker who signed from Falkirk in 1989. John Gallacher found it difficult to live up to his more celebrated namesake. United were rebuilding for the future and Gallacher just didn't fit into the plans. Between 1989 and 1992 he made 27 appearances and scored seven goals with a further seven appearances as a substitute.

GARBUTT, JOHN. Scarborough-born goalkeeper who signed for the club via non-League side Billingham in 1939. Garbutt made a total of 53 appearances for United but his career was badly disrupted by the war.

GARDNER, ALEC. Strong, sensible defender who arrived at Newcastle from Leith Athletic. Gardner was hugely influential in the building of the United side as the club moved into the twentieth century. Alec Gardner would control the United defence with clever footwork and clear instructions, producing calm and confidence. He made some 313 appearances and scored 26 times.

GARDNER, DAVID. Another full-back who proved his worth, Dave Gardner was more of a workhorse; with strength in the tackle and a hefty boot, he was capable of breaking down most attacks with his no-nonsense style of play. He made 78 appearances and scored two goals between 1899 and 1902.

GARNHAM, ALF. Slight-built full-back who made 50 appearances for the club and scored one goal between 1934 and 1939.

GARROW, HERBERT. Signed professional terms for the club in February 1960 having been spotted playing for Irish side, Fochabers. Garrow was just 18 when he came to United but sadly he never instilled confidence in his defence and managed just four first-team appearances between 1960 and 1963.

GASCOIGNE, PAUL. Gateshead-born United star, Gazza was one of the most gifted footballers to grace a United shirt. His wit and intelligence on the ball was a marvel to behold. Gascoigne could do things with a football the likes of which had never before been seen in England. He made his Newcastle debut in 1985 and went on to make 95 appearances and score 25 goals. He made a further nine appearances as a substitute.

A player of undoubted quality, Gascoigne could also frustrate. Perhaps it was the recklessness of youth, or just a lack of experience. Every so often he would commit some outrageous act which would attract the wrong kind of attention, be it on or off the field. Despite this, everybody loved him. Gazza was a hero from home, a Geordie, someone who the fans could relate to – a real character.

Transferred to Tottenham Hotspur in 1988, Gazza is perhaps the son the city of Newcastle would most like to come home. Despite an injury-hit career in Italy there was a rush for his signature when he announced his intention to return to Britain. Rangers won the race with a fee of almost £5,000,000. This could well be for the betterment of our football as Gazza will have matured and may well feel he has something to prove.

Paul Gascoigne

GAYLE, HOWARD. Loan signing in the 1982–83 season, Howard Gayle was a forward officially on Liverpool's books. He made eight appearances and scored two goals before signing for Birmingham in January 1983. He was a tall, lumbering giant but a proven goalscorer.

GHEE, TOMMY. Wing-half who signed from St Mirren in 1897. Similar in attitude and style to Alec Gardner, Ghee went on to make 140 appearances and score three goals for the club between 1897 and 1902.

GIBB, TOMMY. Dark-haired midfielder Tommy Gibb arrived at St James's Park from Partick Thistle in August 1968. A terrier in the middle of the park, Gibb was one of the main powerhouses of the United team. European honours soon came his way in the Inter Cities Fairs Cup. Gibb was one of those players who just oozed confidence, seldom did he put a foot wrong, and when he did he was the first to make amends. He made no less than 234 appearances, 12 more as a substitute, and scored 16 goals in competitive matches for United. Gibb and Moncur were a formidable partnership; few could better them in Europe. He transferred to Sunderland in June 1985.

GIBSON, COLIN. The outside-right Colin Gibson, with one England 'B' international cap, signed in July 1948 after hostilities had ended. He had previously played for Cardiff City. Made 24 appearances and scored five goals in 1948–49 before being sold to Aston Villa.

GIBSON, JIM. Irish-born forward who was signed from Linfield in January 1959, Jim Gibson was not to feature too heavily in United's development. He made two appearances and scored one goal between 1959 and 1961 and later played for Cambridge United and Luton Town.

GIBSON, WILLIAM. Left-half midfielder Willie Gibson was signed from Scottish club Ayr United in 1923. He was a fine footballer who possessed intricate ball skills and could read the game with an unerring eye. Gibson played 142 games for United and scored four goals. One newspaper report of the era called him 'a real gem'.

GILFILLAN, ROBERT. This forward arrived via Cowdenbeath in October 1959 and remained at the club for just one season, 1959–60. Gilfillan made seven appearances and scored two goals. He was released and moved first to Raith Rovers and then to Southend United. He was a rather ordinary forward with little to make him stand out from the rest.

GILLESPIE, KEITH. Signed as part of the deal which took Andy Cole to Manchester United. Kevin Keegan stated that Gillespie was an integral part of the transfer. He is a youngster with a great deal of talent who, as a flying winger, can leave an opponent in his wake with a jink of his hips. One to watch for the future.

GILLESPIE, WILLIAM. Ex-East Fife full-back, Gillespie made nine appearances for the club between 1927 and 1929.

GINOLA, DAVID. David Ginola was signed from Paris St Germain in July 1995 for a fee of £2.5 million. Widely tipped to become one of the top stars in United's team, he is certain to prove his worth in the Premiership. As a youngster, Ginola was turned down by Nice but was snapped up instead by Toulon, where his ability was highly rated. From there he moved on to the now defunct Matra Racing and followed this with a spell at Brest. He signed for PSG in 1991 after Brest were also declared bankrupt. It was with the Paris club that Ginola captured the soccer world's attentions, playing some outstanding football in his European Cup matches of 1994–95. Ginola made his French international debut against Albania in November 1990 and his skill has impressed ever since. He will undoubtedly set St James's Park alight with his neat footwork and delightful passing abilities.

GOALKEEPERS. In a fixture against West Ham on 21 April 1986, Newcastle fielded three different goalkeepers. First-team keeper Martin Thomas was carried off injured. His replacement, Chris Hedworth, also went off, and Peter Beardsley was forced to don the keeper's jersey. Curiously, Alvin Martin, the West Ham centre-half, scored one goal against each of the three keepers. The result was a forgettable 8–1 defeat!

GOALS. Most goals scored by United in one season: 98 in Division One in 1951–52.

GOALS. Most league goals scored by an individual: 177 scored by Jackie Milburn between 1946 and 1957.

GOALS. Most league and cup goals scored by an individual; 200 scored by Jackie Milburn between 1946 and 1957.

GOALS. Most league goals scored by an individual in one season; 36 scored by Hugh Gallacher in 1926/27 season.

GOALS. Most league and cup goals scored by an individual in one season; 41 by Andy Cole 1993/94 season.

GOALS. Most goals scored by an individual in one match: 6 scored by Len Shackleton v Newport C, October 1946.

GOALS. Quickest goal ever recorded: 5 seconds; scored by Malcolm Macdonald who had the ball passed to him direct from kick-off and launched it over the St Johnstone goalkeeper's head in a 1975 pre-season friendly at Muirfield Park, Perth.

GODDARD, PAUL. A player who fitted in well at the club, Goddard was signed from West Ham in 1986 and was seen as a proven goalscorer. Sadly, Paul, although liking the club, had played all of his football in the south and it was this which drew him away from St James's Park. Goddard made 70 appearances and scored 23 times for United before moving to Derby County, Millwall and Ipswich Town, where he remains on the coaching staff. A likeable sort of player who never let the club down.

GOODWILL, THOMAS. Midfield player between 1913 and 1916. Tommy Goodwill was killed in the war in 1916 whilst serving with the Northumberland Fusiliers. He made 60 appearances and scored seven goals.

GORDON, JAMES. Jimmy Gordon was a marvellous servant to Newcastle United. He joined the club from Wishaw Juniors and was a real stalwart in the United defence. His tenacity was matched by his apparent comfort on the ball – Gordon never seemed troubled. He went on to make 143 competitive match appearances and scored three goals. He made a further 111 wartime appearances and scored 18 goals for Newcastle between 1935 and 1945. He later played for Middlesbrough.

GOSNALL, ALBERT. A 12-stone, 5'10" outside-left who signed from Southern League club Chatham. Gosnall was a real professional and had an appetite for extra training and fine-tuning his ball skills. Between 1904 and 1910 he made 124 appearances and scored 18 goals.

GOWLING, ALAN. Huge striker who was prepared to put his head where only fools and angels dare. Gowling was a brave striker whose career had started at Manchester United, then flourished at Huddersfield Town, before signing for Newcastle in August 1975. The tall, well-built centre-forward scored most of his goals through absolute bravery, launching himself head-first at any ball which remotely appeared to be coming his way. His style of play was best described as 'unorthodox'. He went on to make 118 appearances and score 48 goals in his three years at the club between 1975 and 1978 before being sold to Bolton Wanderers where he continued to score.

GRAHAM, W. Tall, lanky central defender who was in United's first-ever League line-up. Between 1892 and 1898 he made some 99 appearances and scored 11 goals for the club.

GREEN, ANTHONY. Small, busy striker whose arrival saw the departure of Keith Dyson. Tony Green had made a name for himself as a tricky inside-forward with Blackpool. He was seen as the ideal man to spark the United attack. A provider of goals rather than a scorer himself, Green, who was 25 when he came to Newcastle, had a bright future ahead of him. This was the move he had been looking for since playing for Albion Rovers – at last a chance to shine for a big club. The chance to shine was, in fact, cut short as Green suddenly became injury-prone. However, he went on

Steve Guppy

to make 33 appearances and score 13 goals between 1971 and 1973 before his football career ended. Without doubt, injuries apart, Green would have made a name for himself in the top flight with United. It was an unfortunate end to a promising career.

GUPPY, STEVE. Steve Guppy joined Newcastle United from Wycombe Wanderers in August 1994 for a fee of £150,000. The midfielder/winger had played a major part in the elevation of Wycombe to the Football League. Unfortunately, after the relative obscurity of non-league football, Guppy never quite lasted at St James's Park and made only a handful of first-team appearances for the club. Before long he was on the move again, this time to Port Vale, where he looks more or less guaranteed to enjoy a regular first-team place.

GUTHRIE, RON. Big Ron Guthrie was an awesome sight in the United defence. He was there to stop players playing, which is no real criticism, as he was one of the best in the country at doing so. Having risen through the juniors, Guthrie broke into the first team in 1963 but did not stake a more permanent claim to the full-back position until the late '60s and early '70s when his real football talent began to show. Between 1963 and 1973 he made 57 appearances (six as a substitute) and scored two goals before a move to Sunderland in January 1973. Guthrie was one of the Sunderland heroes of 1973 when they beat Leeds United 1–0 in the Cup final, with Guthrie being recognised as one of the outstanding performers in their team.

H

HADDOCK, PETER. Having signed professional terms for his home-town club in December 1979, the lean Haddock was a bright prospect who fell foul of injury. A defender with pace and a delightful pass, he made 61 first-team outings, four more as a substitute. Injury curtailed his Newcastle career and he transferred to Leeds United where he went on to make over 100 further appearances for the Yorkshire side before retiring through injury.

HAIR, GEORGE. As an outside-left signed in 1943, Hair was something of a wily character on the ball. Quick though a little ungainly, he made 26 appearances and bagged eight goals between 1943 and 1949.

HALE, KEN. Hale, a striker with a keen eye for the target, was a local player born in Blyth and signed for United's juniors. He turned professional in October 1956 and scored 16 goals in 35 matches before a move to Coventry City in December 1962.

HALL, THOMAS. Centre-forward who signed from Sunderland in 1913 for a fee of £425. Hall had made a big impact on Wearside and had played a major role in the

Championship-winning season of 1912–13. At Newcastle he made 54 appearances between 1913 and 1920 and scored 16 goals – not quite as outstanding as he was with Sunderland.

HALLIDAY, BRUCE. An apprentice who signed as a professional in January 1979, Halliday made a total of 38 appearances for the club, scoring once. He was sold as a defender to Darlington in September 1982.

HAMPSON, WILLIAM. This wonderfully reliable full-back, was 32 years of age when he signed from Norwich City in January 1914 for a fee of £1,250. Hampson went on to make 174 appearances for United, scoring one goal. He appeared in the victorious 1924 FA Cup final when Villa were defeated 2–0. Hampson was at that time the oldest player to win an FA Cup-winners' medal – he was aged 41 years and 8 months!

He later went on to a marvellous career in club management with Carlisle, Ashington and Leeds United. He has proven to be an excellent club servant wherever he has been.

HANNAH, GEORGE. A remarkable player, well ahead of his time, George Hannah was born in Liverpool but began his football career with Irish club side Linfield. Signed for Newcastle in January 1949, this courageous inside-forward went on to become an Irish international. He made 167 outings for the Magpies, scoring 41 goals. He transferred to Lincoln City in September 1957.

HARDWICK, STEVE. England youth international goalkeeper, the Mansfield-born Hardwick joined another local-league side, Chesterfield. Arrived at St James's Park in December 1976 and went on to make 101 first-team appearances. Hardwick was, if anything, stocky and a little slow at getting down to low balls. He moved to Oxford United in February 1983 and made a brief comeback playing for non-League side Kettering Town, but sustained a horrific back injury in a pre-season friendly when he tumbled head over heels as he challenged for a cross. This was typical of his bravery throughout his career.

HARFORD, MICK. A robust, gangly centre-forward, Mick Harford is a footballer who gives his all in every game. At the time of writing (1995) he is still playing and scoring for Premier League side Wimbledon.

Born in Sunderland, Harford's first League club was Lincoln City, before United spotted his talents and brought him to Tyneside in December 1980. He made 18 appearances, one more as a substitute, and scored four goals to repay United's faith. He moved to Bristol City before settling down at Birmingham City. What Mick Harford does not have in skill he more than compensates for with heart and commitment.

HARRIS, JOE. A left-half signed from Middlesbrough in 1925, Harris was a fair-haired Scottish international. Despite making 157 appearances and scoring twice in his spell at the club, between 1925 and 1931, Harris never truly held down a firm place in the first team. In the 1927 Championship-winning side he made nine full appearances. Having said that, his talent was certainly put to good use by the club, and few could deny his competence during any one of his outings.

HARRIS, NEIL. Although hardly the biggest centre-forward United have ever had, Neil Harris was certainly one of the most consistent. In a five-year spell between signing in 1920 and leaving in 1925, he scored 101 goals in 194 appearances. Harris was a shoot-on-sight type of striker but to give him his due he was very successful with this strategy.

He scored many important goals for the club, none more so than the opening goal in the 2–0 1994 FA Cup final victory over Aston Villa. This was a cracking shot rifled home from six yards, leaving the Villa keeper standing as the ball flew past him. Harris had a first-class rapport with fellow United forward, Stan Seymour, and together the pair terrorised defences up and down England.

HARVEY, BRIAN. London-born goalkeeper who was signed from non-League Wisbech in September 1958. Harvey was a splendid keeper who went on to make 91 appearances between 1958 and 1961.

Although initially signed as cover for United's regular first-team keeper, Simpson, Harvey did well, but with the arrival of Welsh International Dave Hollins his days were numbered. He moved to non-League Cambridge City before returning to League soccer with Blackpool.

HARVEY, JOHN. A forward who was in the twilight years of his football career when he joined United in 1897 from Sunderland. He made 31 first-team outings and scored eight goals between 1897 and 1899. He was a useful sort of player whose experience was utilised to guide younger colleagues.

HARVEY, JOSEPH. A player synonymous with Newcastle United, Joe Harvey achieved so many great things in his time at the club as both player and manager.

Started his career as a professional with Bradford before moving to Wolves and then Bournemouth. A solid defender, he liked to get stuck into the thick of the action.

After the war he joined Newcastle (October 1945) for a £4,250 fee. In the next eight years he rose to become team captain and led the side back into Division 1 and lifted the FA Cup twice in 1951 and 1952. In 1953 he retired from playing and was made team coach until 1955. Harvey then left to learn his managerial skills at clubs such as Workington and Barrow before returning to St James's Park in June 1962. He assembled a Division 2 Championship-winning side in the 1964-65 season and took the club on to European honours. Unfortunately, after a dire FA Cup final defeat in 1974, Harvey lost a great deal of credibility with the fans. There were calls for his resignation, with claims that he was a dinosaur in a young man's game. In May 1975 he resigned as team manager, a position the club struggled to fill with any great confidence until the arrival of Kevin Keegan. Joe Harvey continued to work for the club under different guises before sadly passing away in February 1989. He made 247 outings for United, scoring 12 goals.

HAY, JAMES. This was an incredible club signing in 1911 as Hay was captain of Celtic and Scotland at the time. Hay was typical of today's midfield players – dominant and a playmaker. His transfer fee of £1,250 was a huge one in 1911, but it was money well spent. Hay went on to make 149 appearances and scored eight goals before leaving the club in 1919.

HEARD, PATRICK. Midfielder signed from Sheffield Wednesday in 1984 who played all of his 34 games in the 1984-85 season. His two goals came against Luton and Ipswich Town. Heard moved on to Middlesbrough in 1985. A player who lacked a certain finesse, Heard was something of a football nomad, playing for nine League sides before he retired.

HENDERSON, JOHN. Goalkeeper who signed from Scottish club side Clyde at the beginning of the 1895–96 season. Although Henderson was in and out of the first team during his two-year stay at St James's Park he managed to make a total of 35 appearances.

HENDRIE, JOHN. Small, stocky forward who has made a career out of scoring goals for each club he has played for. Hendrie is not an outstanding footballer but is very proficient at what he does. He made 34 appearances during the 1988–89 season before being sold to Leeds United. He scored four goals for United and is still scoring them for Middlesbrough.

HESLOP, GEORGE. Wallsend-born Heslop made his name in non-League circles as a towering centre-half. United signed him from Dudley Welfare in February 1959 and he went on to make 32 appearances on Tyneside before being released to Everton in March 1962.

HEWISON, ROBERT. Right-half who was born at Backworth and signed for United from Whitley Athletic. During his first era at the club, 1908–14, he never managed to get into the first team. He returned in December 1919, however, and progressed to make 70 first-team appearances.

After retiring from the game through injury he moved into management with Northampton, QPR and Bristol City. He then moved into scouting, having been found guilty of making illegal payments to players. Eventually returned to management with Bath City before bowing out of the game completely in 1961.

HIBBERT, WILLIAM. England international centre-forward-cum-utility player, Hibbert was signed for £1,950 from Bury. He was a slightly-built player who had a lovely touch and was quick to react to opportunities in and around the penalty area. He made 155 appearances, scoring 49 goals between 1911 and 1920.

HIBBITT, TERRY. A midfield player with an exquisite left foot, Terry Hibbitt was a gift from Leeds United for whom he had struggled to maintain a first-team place. He came to Tyneside in the first instance in August 1971 and proved himself to be a workhorse who could prise open the best defences with his stupendous passing. He was sold to Birmingham in August 1975. Hibbitt returned to Newcastle in May 1978. The Bradford-born player fell in love with life in the North East and made a career total of 258 appearances for the club, was a substitute just once and managed to score 13 goals. Hibbitt was a firm favourite with fans. His untimely death in August 1994 aged just 46 touched more than a few hearts. He was highly respected as a man as well as a footballer. He will be deeply missed by all who knew him and all those who can remember him as a player.

HIGGINS, ANDREW. Signed in 1905, this centre-forward from Kilmarnock was a slow starter but once he made his breakthrough into the first team, he proved himself a talent to match those who had gone before him. Some startling performances ensured that Higgins received international recognition for Scotland. In a 14–year spell between 1905 and 1919 he made 150 appearances and scored 41 goals.

HIGGINS, BILL. Bill Higgins was an experienced professional who had played in central defence for several clubs including Bristol City. Between 1898 and 1900 he made 39 appearances and scored three goals for United.

HILL, JACK. This flame-haired, 6'2" centre-half had clashed on several occasions with United's own Hughie Gallacher. Indeed the latter had got no change from Hill who was classed as one of the few defenders who could contain Hughie. Hill cost what was then a British transfer record fee of £8,100 and was immediately made team captain. An outstanding player of his era, Hill went on to make 78 appearances for Newcastle. He scored two goals.

HILL, JAMES. Northern Ireland international forward signed from Linfield in July 1957. He made 11 appearances and scored twice in 1957–58 before transferring to Norwich City in August 1958.

HILLEY, DAVID. Third Lanark inside-forward who attracted the attention of several English clubs, but who signed for United in August 1962. Hilley was a bright prospect and made several U-23 Scottish international appearances. Went on to play 209 first-class matches, scoring 33 goals for United.

HOCKEY, TREVOR. The rock-hard midfielder and Welsh international Hockey was renowned for his brusque attitude on the pitch. Signed by United in November 1963, Trevor went on to make 56 appearances and score three goals before moving to Birmingham in November 1965. Hockey was one of several players of the '60s and '70s who were renowned as 'choppers'. Yet Hockey had more to his game than taking players' legs away; he could pass and shoot with some accuracy and had a heart as big as St James's Park.

HODGES, GLYN. Stocky front player who came to Tyneside with high expectations, but a lack of consistent form meant his stay was brief. Hodges all too often drifted out of games. He was not a ball-winner but a ball-player, which seemed to let him down. Hodges, when on form, has a remarkable touch and has matured into a fine player for Sheffield United. He spent just one season at Newcastle, 1987–88, playing seven games without scoring.

HOLLINS, DAVID. Welsh international keeper signed in March 1961 who made 121 appearances in a six-season spell with the club. He moved to Mansfield Town in February 1967. Hollins was a tremendous 'reaction' keeper who occasionally had difficulties with the odd cross. Goal-keeping errors always seem worse than those of outfield players. Hollins never made too many, but, as a keeper, one is too many!

HOOPER, MIKE. Goalkeeper Mike Hooper, signed from Liverpool, is now playing as understudy to Srnicek, just as he did at Anfield when he played second-fiddle to Grobbelaar. Hooper has always performed proficiently but is prone to what seem to be lapses in concentration. Despite this problem he has proved to be a good deputy keeper.

HOTTIGER, MARC. A Swiss international, Hottiger has grown in confidence since his arrival at St James's Park in the summer of 1994. As a right-back he enjoys nothing more than an overlapping run down the wing. Best remembered for a terrific strike against Blackburn Rovers in January 1995.

HOUGHTON, FRANK. Born in Preston in 1926, Houghton made a name for himself as an industrious wing-half. His talents took him to Ireland's Ballymena. In December 1947 he signed as a professional for Newcastle and made 57 appearances with a reasonable return of ten goals. He was sold to Exeter in August 1954.

HOWARD, PATRICK. If awards were given for dedication and downright stubbornness, then Pat Howard would win several. This likeable defender, signed from Barnsley in September 1971, staked a claim for a first-team spot and refused to give it up. Howard saw off several pretenders to

Marc Hottiger

his throne. Sandy-haired, lean and agile, his tackling was first class and his distribution second to none. In all, he made 224 appearances (two more as a substitute) and scored eight goals. He was sold to Arsenal in September 1976.

HOWEY, STEVE. Tall central defender currently earning an excellent reputation for himself as a ball-winner and stopper. Howey has matured since he broke into the United team in 1989 and will hopefully continue to earn more

89

praise from United fans and football critics alike. Born in Sunderland, he is one of the new breed whose genuine love for the club ensures 100% commitment.

HOWIE, JAMES. Howie was signed from Bristol Rovers at the beginning of the 1903–4 season. Howie was a swift-moving, silky-skilled inside-forward who was instrumental in much of United's attacking prowess for some seven years. He made 235 appearances and bagged 83 goals.

HUDSON, RAY. Born in Gateshead, Hudson joined United as an apprentice and was groomed as a midfield player, a position for which United already had a glut of quality, thus making it difficult for Hudson to make a name for himself. In the end he made 20 appearances, five more as a substitute and scored two goals between 1973 and 1978, before returning to relative obscurity.

HUDSPETH, FRANK. Another of United's all-time greats, Frank Hudspeth played for the club he loved. Although he managed just one solitary appearance in an England shirt, he made a fantastic 472 appearances for Newcastle United, scoring 37 goals, the majority of which were from the penalty spot. In fact, no other United player has converted so many spot-kicks. Hudspeth collected an FA Cup-winners' medal in 1924 and a League Championship medal in 1927. A truly dedicated full-back, Hudspeth was something of a disciplinarian who lived for his football.

HUGHES, GORDON. As a winger signed from Tow Law Town in August 1956, Hughes suffered from indifferent form; one minute brilliant, the next he seemed to hide. He was an honest, hard-working player, but, as with all wingers, everything had to be just right for a mazy run or an unbelievable gallop and cross. Hughes made 143 appearances for Newcastle and scored 20 goals between 1956 and 1963, when he moved to Derby County.

HUNT, ANDREW. Hunt was signed by Ossie Ardiles from non-League outfit Kettering Town, when they were desperate for money and almost bankrupt. Hunt was a tall, lean forward who hailed from Kings Lynn. He seemed a little lazy at times, but could perform brilliantly when least expected. In a two-year spell between 1991 and 1993 he made 39 appearances (nine more as a substitute) and scored 13 goals. He now plays for West Bromwich Albion where he is a regular goalscorer.

HUTCHISON, DUNCAN. Centre-forward Hutchison arrived from Dundee United having scored 40 goals in one season for the club. The talk in the town was that Hutchison had come to replace Hugh Gallacher. Wee Hughie would have none of it; he wasn't about to relinquish his jersey to some young whippersnapper. Hutchison soon earned himself a good reputation on Tyneside. He ran like the wind and worked very hard as a centre-forward. The local media provided him with the nickname 'Hurricane Hutch' and soon a new hero was wearing the black-and-white striped shirt. Hutchison's reign lasted just three years. Between 1929 and 1932, when he made 46 appearances and netted 21 goals.

I

ILEY, JAMES. A talented wing-half, Jim Iley joined United from Nottingham Forest in September 1962, aged 27. An England U-23 international and a representative of the Football League side, Iley's career began at Sheffield United before a £16,000 move to Spurs, then a similarly priced move to Forest. United gave £17,000 for his services and Iley certainly repaid their faith in him.

A well-built player, he was not one of the swiftest movers. His constructive ideas and movement into space, however, more than compensated for this. He played 243 games with six more appearances as a substitute, scoring 16 goals for the club, before moving to Peterborough United as player-manager in January 1969. Iley seemed to enjoy his football. His face held a permanent smile and he always made time to speak to supporters. He was one of the game's gentlemen.

IMRIE, WILLIAM. There can rarely have been a more intimidating-looking footballer. Bill Imrie – bright red hair, 6'2″ and weighing in at over 14 stone – was a £6,500 acquisition from Blackburn Rovers. An ex-Scottish international, Imrie was not just capable of frightening the opposition; behind that permanent grimace and snarling accent was a wing-half who knew his football. Imrie's well-placed and, one has to say, powerful headers were pinpoint accurate. His huge frame was incredibly agile as he often slipped past a lunging tackle as he charged forward.

Imrie joined United as the club were slipping out of Division 1. He remained at St James's Park from 1934 until 1938, and made 128 appearances, scoring 24 times – not a bad goal count for a defender. Off the field Imrie was anything but oppressive; he could be seen chatting to supporters before and after games and liked nothing more than greeting his young fans.

INGLIS, R. This squad player made just three appearances in United's first-ever League season. It would seem that he was one of several players used as a stop-gap in a bid to find the strongest first team in the 1893–94 season.

INNERD, WILLIAM. Bill Innerd played only three games for the club, one of which was in the 1905 Championship season. Innerd's period at the club lasted from 1900 until the 1904–05 season, when he signed for Crystal Palace.

INTERNATIONALS. The following is a list of players who have made full international appearances for their respective countries whilst playing for Newcastle.

ENGLAND
P. Beardsley, 18
I. A. Broadis, 6
J. Carr, 2
D. Fairhurst, 1
A. A. Gosnell, 1
J. H. Hill, 3
F. C. Hudspeth, 1
M. Kingsley, 1
R. Lee, 1
M. Macdonald, 14
J. E. T. Milburn, 13
J. R. Richardson, 2
J. Rutherford, 11
A. Shepherd, 1

C. W. Spencer, 2
J. Stewart, 1
B. Venison, 1
C. C. M. Veitch, 6
C. R. Waddle, 8
S. Weaver, 3
J. D. Wright, 1

EIRE
J. Anderson, 11
D. T. Kelly, 4
L. O'Brien, 3
K. Sheedy, 4
L. Tuohy, 2

NORTHERN IRELAND
T. Casey, 10
T. Cassidy, 20
J. Cowan, 1
D. J. Craig, 25
K. Gillespie, 2
R. M. Keith, 23
W. McCracken, 8
D. McCreery, 19
W. S. McFaul, 5
A. McMichael, 40
M. A. O'Neill, 10
W. E. Ross, 1
I. Stewart, 9
T. J. Wright, 15

SCOTLAND
A. Aitken, 8
R. Aitken, 6
R. F. D. Ancell, 2
J. M. Boyd, 1
F. Brennan, 7
W. D. Cowan, 1
T. B. Craig, 1
H. K. Gallacher, 13
A. Green, 2

N. Harris, 1
J. Hay, 4
A. Higgins, 4
J. Howie, 3
J. Lawrence, 1
W. L. Low, 5
R. S. McColl, 1
A. McCombie, 2
R. McKay, 1
P. McWilliam, 8
R. C. Mitchell, 2
R. Moncur, 16
R. Orr, 2
R. Templeton, 3
G. W. Wilson, 1

WALES
I. J. Allchurch, 12
A. D. Burton, 7
A. Davies, 1
E. R. Davies, 6
R. W. Davies, 11
W. I. Foulkes, 11
G. Hodges, 1
D. M. Hollins, 11
G. Lowrie, 1
A. B. Neilson, 1
M. R. Thomas, 1

INVASIONS. The year – 1901; the fixture – a Division 2 clash with local rivals and division leaders, Sunderland. St James's Park was filled to the rafters, with an estimated 50,000 to 70,000 people making their way to the ground, which could officially only hold 30,000 at the time! The gates were locked a full 45 minutes before kick-off. Outside, people were still making their way to the ground. It was mayhem.

Suddenly, like an army on the march, the turnstile gates were systematically broken down by the enthusiastic crowd clamouring to get in to see their heroes. These people were not criminals, just fans desperately keen to get inside. The sheer weight of numbers was a recipe for disaster. Thousands continued to force their way into the ground. Fences collapsed as fans scurried for the tiniest space. Hundreds climbed onto the roof of the main stand. It was a nightmare. With no room on the terraces, fans were forced to surround the pitchside. Eventually, at around 3.30 p.m., the referee appeared, took one look at the pandemonium and called off the match! This was the spark which ignited the worst scenes of hooliganism at St James's Park for many years to come. Goalposts were torn down, as was the club flag. Missiles were hurled by opposing sets of supporters. Women and children screamed in terror. The rioting continued until well after 4.30 p.m. and it was not until around an hour later that the ground was cleared. It was incredible that no one died in the mayhem. In fact, only 15 people were injured; one of them an idiot who had fallen from the roof of the main stand!

Another sad day in United's history occurred again at St James's Park when Nottingham Forest were the visitors in a 1974 FA Cup quarter-final game. The United crowd were rampant, ready for Cup glory. However, things were not going well. A volatile atmosphere was made worse by what the home crowd saw as some appalling refereeing decisions. United were already losing 2–1 when Pat Howard gave away a penalty and was sent off. The United throng were in uproar, the Leazes End swayed and fans screamed their disgust at the match official. Forest duly scored from the spot-kick and went 3–1 up. A few Forest fans, gathered in the Gallowgate, leapt onto the pitch as though goading the Leazes End. The Leazes End fans were not slow to react and hundreds of them spilled out onto the pitch and ran towards the away fans in the Gallowgate. It looked like a battle scene from the film *Zulu*. The players were escorted from the pitch while the police took control of the situation. During the fracas which followed a number of officers received minor injuries and it took a full 20 minutes to restore order and restart the game. Eventually, to finish off a dramatic afternoon, United came back to win 4–3, only for the result to be declared void and a replay ordered. United eventually won through 1–0.

J

JACKSON, DARREN. This Scottish-born striker made a name for himself with his scoring prowess for Meadowbank Thistle. The slimline Jackson was rather lightweight when he arrived at the club in 1986. His scoring touch suddenly disappeared as the pressures of a higher standard of football began to tell. Jackson made 63 appearances, 16 more as a substitute and scored nine goals. United released him in 1988 when he joined Dundee United and duly got back into the habit of scoring. Since then he has transferred to Hibernian, where he continues to score regularly, and has won a couple of Scottish caps.

JACKSON, JOHN. A defender who was brought in from Glasgow Rangers, Jackson was a reliable chap and a consistent performer in the United defence. He won a Division 2 Championship medal with the club in 1898 and made a total of 64 appearances between 1897 and 1899, scoring two goals.

JACKSON, PETER. Born in Bradford, Peter Jackson joined his local league club in 1978. A midfielder-cum-striker, he possessed no small amount of crafty skill. He was signed by Newcastle in the 1986–87 season and remained at the club until 1988, during which time he made 69 appearances and scored three goals. Jackson returned to Bradford City before a move to Huddersfield Town in 1990.

JEFFERY, HAROLD. This defender, who played between 1892 and 1897, had signed for the newly formed club after the demise of Newcastle West End. Jeffery played in United's first-ever League fixture and scored three goals in 48 appearances.

JEFFREY, MICHAEL. Tall, lean striker who was signed from the depths of the new-style Division 3 and Doncaster Rovers for a cut-price fee of £85,000 in October 1993, Jeffrey seems a real bargain. Alert and keen, he has yet to break into the first team on a regular basis, with only a handful of appearances to date. Jeffrey may well prove to be yet another shrewd signing by Kevin Keegan.

JOBEY, GEORGE. A £10 signing from Morpeth Harriers in May 1906, Jobey was a sturdy half-back who made some 53 appearances for United, scoring two goals between 1906 and 1913. United sold him to Woolwich Arsenal for £500, an amazing profit. He later went into club management and was successful with Wolves and Derby County. After a life suspension from the game for paying players illegal bonuses, he moved into the hotel trade. However, the suspension was lifted and Mansfield tempted him back into football management. It was a sad liaison; Jobey remained with the Stags for 16 months before being sacked for 'having no interest'! Jobey was a strict disciplinarian but was well respected by those who knew him. He died at his Derby home in 1962.

JOHNSON, PETER. Born in Harrogate, Johnson created something of a sensation with his performances in local youth leagues, so much so that Middlesbrough took a gamble on him. Johnson signed professional terms at Ayresome Park in October 1976 and made 42 appearances, scoring one goal, before a move to Newcastle in October 1980.

A stylish defender, Johnson found himself playing more reserve-team football. Between 1980 and 1983 he made just 20 appearances for the Magpies. He was released to Bristol City in the 1982–83 season, before a return north to Doncaster and then Darlington.

K

KEEBLE, VICTOR. Signed from Colchester United in February 1952, Keeble was a hugely dominant centre-forward who could overpower defenders with his strength and aerial power. Keeble had a terrific header on him; at least one goalkeeper at the time said it was as powerful as some players' shots!

Keeble made 120 appearances and scored in 67 of these games. His workrate and goal-power ranks him alongside the very best of the United 'superstrikers'. He was sold to West Ham in October 1957.

KEEGAN, KEVIN. Just how many individuals can affect the attendances at football grounds all over the country? Very few I can tell you. But Kevin Keegan is one of those who can. As a player he filled stadiums all over the world as football followers eagerly paid their admission to see his exquisite talents. Keegan was a genius, he alone transformed Newcastle United into what they are today. He spent two years as a player on Tyneside, 1982–1984, making 85 appearances and scoring 49 goals.

When he returned as manager in February 1992 he took the club by the scruff of the neck and dragged it to its feet. Promotion back to the Premier League soon followed.

Backed by the club's main benefactor, Sir John Hall, the pair have worked in tandem to bring success back to St James's Park. Signings such as that of Andy Cole, have ensured that United can at last be one of the 'Big Boys' in the transfer market. Granted, the Cole deal was a gamble: £7,000,000 plus interest, plus Keith Gillespie, but I think Keegan has played a masterful hand. With money in the bank and a team who continue to win, United may well have it all. A trophy can only be just around the corner.

For the record Keegan's achievements are as follows; England International, 63 caps, U-23 International, 5 caps. European Cup Winner, 1977, runner-up 1980, UEFA Cup winner, 1973, 1976, Footballer of the Year, 1976, European

Kevin Keegan

Footballer of the Year, 1978, 1979, Bundesliga Footballer of the Year, 1978, Football League Champion, 1973, 1976, 1977, Bundesliga Champion, 1978, FA Cup winner, 1974, runner-up 1977, Division 1 Champion, 1993, OBE, 1982. What more can one say!

KEELEY, GLEN. Essex-born defender Glen Keeley was tall and lanky, giving the impression that he was about to topple over at any minute. In fact, he was finely balanced and perfectly comfortable with the ball at his feet, although he preferred it on his head. Signed from Ipswich Town in August 1972, his stay in the North East lasted until 1976. During this period he made 61 appearances and scored four goals. He also appeared as a substitute on one occasion. He was sold to Blackburn Rovers in August 1976 and became a mainstay of their side for six years.

KEERY, STANLEY. A wing-half from Shrewsbury Town, Keery made 19 outings in United colours and scored one goal. He spent 1952–56 at St James's Park before moving to Mansfield Town, where he performed with a good deal more consistency.

KEITH, RICHARD. Richard Keith was bought from Linfield in September 1956. A solid full-back, he quickly earned himself a first-team position and worked hard at keeping it. Keith made a total of 223 appearances for the club between 1956 and 1964, scoring two goals. He was a Northern Ireland international who represented his country on three occasions. He moved to Bournemouth in February 1964, before passing away at the relatively young age of 34. Dick Keith was a marvellous servant to Newcastle United; few players display the loyalty to one club which he clearly showed.

KELLY, DAVID. Bustling and spritely centre-forward David Kelly was worshipped during his stay at Newcastle. He made 79 appearances and scored 38 goals – no mean return for the youngster who began his career with Walsall in 1983. Kelly was signed from Leicester City in 1991 and nowadays scores goals for Wolves. His hat-trick against Cambridge United in the 1992–93 season was a pleasure to watch, as was a further hat-trick in the 7–1 demolition of Leicester that same season. 'David Kelly on the Telly' was not half as good as Kelly in real life!

KELLY, GARY. Goalkeeper who arrived as an apprentice and broke into the first team in the 1986–87 season. Kelly lacked that special something which makes certain keepers stand out. He was agile enough but often seemed to labour and get himself into all kinds of muddles. In 1988–89 he was loaned out to Blackpool but returned after just five games at Bloomfield Road. He made 60 first-team appearances for United before being sold to Bury in 1989.

KELLY, PETER. Another Scottish defender, Kelly was signed as an apprentice and turned professional in July 1974. To be honest, he was never truly outstanding and was occasionally caught out by the odd speedy winger. Kelly made 35 appearances, with two more as a substitute, between 1974 and 1981.

KENNEDY, ALAN. The Sunderland-born England international defender Alan Kennedy had a distinguished career in the game, which began at Newcastle United. Signed professional in September 1972, he went on to make 194 appearances for United, five more as a substitute, and score nine goals. His superb performance in the 1974 FA Cup final against Liverpool was a factor in the Anfield side signing him some four years later. By then Kennedy had matured into one of the best defenders in world football. He went on to score goals in the 1981 and 1984 European Cup finals for Liverpool. A dedicated professional, he returned to the North East and Sunderland, but after his success at Anfield it was a bit of an anti-climax. Despite this, Kennedy gave his all, and his 40-yard curler against Carlisle United at Roker Park is probably the classiest goal he ever scored.

KERRAY, JAMES. Jim Kerray, an inside-forward, was signed from Huddersfield Town in April 1967. He remained at the club until 1963 and made a total of 40 appearances, scoring ten goals. Injuries dogged his career, but he was a tricky front-runner with a capable shot.

KETTLEBOROUGH, KEITH. A much-travelled forward who played for United for just one season, 1965–66, in which he made 33 appearances without a goal. It was probably this which forced United to release him in December 1966, to Doncaster Rovers as a player-manager. Prior to joining United, Kettleborough had appeared for Rotherham and Sheffield United.

KILCLINE, BRIAN. Thick-set central-defender Kilcline looked mean with his permed locks and Mexican-style moustache creating an intimidating appearance. Kilcline was a tough player who expected everyone else to be as tough as he was. Commitment was his favourite word. I cannot recall Kilcline shirking a responsibility in his time with the club. He made a total of 24 appearances with 16 as a substitute between 1992 and 1994 before he was sold to Swindon Town.

KING, JOHN. Striker who was signed from Partick Thistle for a fee of £600 in 1913. King was a spritely player with good pace and a good touch, but unfortunately he lacked the courage of his convictions. Dodgy tackles were not for him. He was rather more an exponent of simple passing and ghosting past defenders. He made 61 appearances and scored ten goals between 1913 and 1920.

KINGSLEY, MATTHEW. The first-ever Newcastle player to receive international recognition for England. Kingsley, a huge goalkeeper, was signed from Lancashire club side Darwen. He made 189 appearances for the Magpies between 1898 and 1904. Press reports of the day often tell how he laid out opposing forwards as he came for crosses, his 14-stone frame clattering into them as he cleared his area with, more often than not, a punched clearance.

KITSON, PAUL. Slenderly-built striker with a huge heart and a great will to do well for Newcastle United. Kitson was

FOOTBALL ASSOCIATION CHALLENGE CUP COMPETITION

FINAL

LIVERPOOL

3

F.A. CUP HONOURS

WINNERS
1965

Runners-up
1914, 1950, 1971

0

NEWCASTLE UNITED

F.A. CUP HONOURS

WINNERS
1910, 1924, 1932,
1951, 1952, 1955

Runners-up
1905, 1906, 1908,
1911

SATURDAY, 4th MAY 1974
Kick-off 3 p.m.

OFFICIAL PROGRAMME

WEMBLEY
STADIUM

FIFTEEN PENCE

1974 FA Cup final programme: Liverpool v Newcastle United

MANCHESTER CITY

SATURDAY, 28th FEBRUARY 1976 · Kick-off 3.30 pm

THE FOOTBALL LEAGUE

CUP FINAL

WEMBLEY STADIUM

Official Souvenir Programme . . . . Twenty pence

NEWCASTLE UNITED

1976 FA Cup final programme: Manchester City v Newcastle United

a proven goalscorer with Derby County and Leicester City before he came to St James's Park. Now seen as a replacement striker for Andy Cole, Kitson is much more than that; he is a different type of player and is more hard-working and more aggressive. Kitson will, I am certain, prove himself to be a goalscorer of some quality in the next few seasons.

KNOX, THOMAS. A left-winger with good control and electric pace, Knox came via Chelsea in February 1965. He made 25 outings for the club, one more as a substitute, and scored one goal before being transferred to Mansfield Town in March 1967.

KOENEN, FRANSISCUS. Dutch U-21 international signed from Nijmegen in August 1980. Koenen struggled to make any impact on the English game, not without the Newcastle crowd willing him to do famously. To be fair to him, he had no idea what he was letting himself in for – British football was vastly different from the Dutch game. He made 13 appearances, one as a substitute, and scored one goal in the 1980–81 season.

KRISTENSEN, BJORN. Danish full international defender who was signed from FC Aarhus in 1988. Kristensen was a quality player and immediately settled into the United side. At 6'1", he was good in the air and had an intelligent football brain. He made 78 appearances, ten more as a substitute, and scored four goals for the club between 1989 and 1993. Kristensen was loaned to Bristol City in the 1992–93 season, where his style of play influenced his old Newcastle boss, Jim Smith, to take him down to Portsmouth.

L

LACKENBY, GEORGE. Newcastle-born full-back who made 19 first-team appearances between 1950 and his 1956 transfer to Exeter City.

LANG, THOMAS. Scottish junior who performed in many outstanding games for the club throughout his eight years on Tyneside with Newcastle. Lang was just 5'7" tall and was an exciting winger. His destruction of the Arsenal full-back, Parker, in the 1932 FA Cup final victory at Wembley, was an astounding piece of wizardry. Lang possessed sensational pace, and was a more than capable goal-getter, scoring 58 times in 229 games between 1926 and 1934.

LAUGHTON, DENNIS. Signed from Greenock Morton in October 1973, Dennis Laughton was a half-back who joined the club as a fringe player. With the possibility of a first-team breakthrough always present, he worked hard at his game but failed to impress team manager Joe Harvey, who released him in 1975. Laughton made just seven first-team appearances in competitive fixtures, plus one more as a substitute.

LAWRENCE, JAMES. This Glaswegian goalkeeper holds the United all-time appearance record, which is unlikely ever to be broken. He played 496 matches (plus 9 Wartime League games) between 1904 and 1922. Lawrence won FA Cup-winners' honours as well as League Champions recognition. International caps arrived not long after. Lawrence was reliable if not spectacular; he always seemed to do the safe thing rather than the dramatic. However, there was the odd lapse in concentration like in the 1911 FA Cup final replay at Old Trafford against Bradford City. City had beaten United in a League fixture just two weeks prior to the final so United had an added incentive to win. A hopeful bouncing ball dropping towards Lawrence in the United goal was hopelessly tame. Jimmy Speirs, the Bradford forward, believed the ball to be going nowhere. He had not allowed for Jimmy Lawrence dropping a clanger! The goalie misjudged the ball and, despite frantic efforts to claw the ball back, it bounced in and United lost the match 1–0.

Yet Lawrence should be remembered for so much more than his one calamitous error. At the tender age of 37 he relinquished the number-one jersey before leaving the club in 1922 and moving into football management with South Shields. A short time later he was offered a similar post with Preston North End, before going abroad where he managed German side Karlsruhe. His return to Britain saw him move to Stranraer as a director where he was eventually made club chairman. Lawrence was a character both on and off the field, and few players are remembered with such genuine affection.

LEACH, TONY. Centre-half signed by Andy Cunningham in 1934. Leach was a tall, wavy-haired centre-half who had plied his trade with Sheffield Wednesday. Aged 31 when he arrived at St James's Park, United could not have expected to get many years' service from him. Indeed, he was brought in to bolster a leaky defence as the club floundered just above the relegation zone. He could not stop the rot, however, as United fell back into Division 2. Leach made some 53 appearances, scoring twice, between 1934 and 1936.

LEAGUE CUP. United have only ever appeared in the final of this competition once; in 1976 against Manchester City, which ended in defeat.

LEAGUE POSITION. Highest. League Champions: Division 1, 1905, 1907, 1909, 1927.

LEAGUE POSITION. Lowest. 1937/38 season; 19th in Division 2. Only avoided relegation to Division 3 North by goal difference! Barnsley, Nottingham Forest and Newcastle all finished the season on 36 points. Barnsley's number of goals against was higher than United's by some 7 goals so Barnsley were relegated.

LEE, GORDON. Gordon Lee had a good career as full-back with Aston Villa, appearing in two League Cup finals in 1962 and 1963 respectively. He moved into coaching with Shrewsbury Town before his first managerial post arrived at Port Vale. January 1974 saw him move to Blackburn Rovers and take them to the Division 3 Championship in the 1974–75 season. Newcastle, in need of a manager, tempted Lee to Tyneside and, in his first season in charge, United made it to the 1976 League Cup final but lost 1–0 to Manchester City. From there on in Lee had an uncomfortable ride at the club. The fans turned against him after the sale of Malcolm Macdonald to Arsenal. To the United faithful it seemed that Lee was getting rid of the stars and building a no-nonsense, average side. In February 1977 he left Newcastle for Everton, a move which caused few complaints around Newcastle.

LEE, ROBERT. A player, who has finally been able to prove his worth. Robert Lee has become one of the most appreciated talents of the last two seasons (1993–94 and 1994–95). Previously, with Charlton Athletic, he always seemed to lack that little extra in the way of finesse. At Newcastle he has found it and is now one of the most complete players in the present-day line-up. An England full international, Lee scored a fine opportunist goal at Wembley for his country. With over 100 United

113

Robert Lee

appearances already registered, Lee can comfortably justify his role in Newcastle's history.

LEIGHTON, WILLIAM. More of a reserve team player, Leighton was given his opportunity in 1932 and greatly impressed everyone who saw him. From Walker Park, he went on to score eight goals in 40 appearances for the club.

LENNOX, MALCOLM. With United between 1895 and 1898, Lennox was signed from Glasgow Perthshire as an out-and-out attacker. Lennox made a total of 49 appearances and scored 18 goals.

LINDSAY, BILLY. Full-back Billy Lindsay was signed from Grimsby Town in 1898. He made 60 appearances and scored one goal between 1898 and 1900 and was influential in bringing the talents of his brother Jimmy to the attention of the United staff.

LINDSAY, DUNCAN. Cowdenbeath striker who joined the club as an ideal replacement for Hughie Gallacher. He cost £2,700, and had been an outstanding scorer in the Scottish game. Lindsay, however, failed to inspire at Newcastle, and although he scored 12 goals in 19 outings, his stay was but a brief one in 1930–31.

LINDSAY, JIMMY. Brother of the more distinguished United player Billy, Jimmy was older and less active for the club, making just two appearances in 1899–1900.

LIVINGSTONE, ARCHIE. Between 1935 and 1938 Livingstone made 33 appearances for the club and scored five goals.

LIVINGSTONE, DUGALD. Dugald Livingstone was manager of the club between December 1954 and January 1956. A full-back, he had played for Celtic, Everton, Plymouth, Aberdeen and Tranmere Rovers. After a brief spell as trainer with Exeter City and Sheffield United, an outstanding managerial career began with Sparta Rotterdam, and continued with the Republic of Ireland, Belgium and then Newcastle United. Livingstone led the club to FA Cup final victory over Manchester City in 1955. The club now looked set to progress into trophy-winning giants. However, as is so often the case, the dream was shattered. Livingstone found that his team selection was questioned by the board and some of the first-team players had not liked his European training methods or style of play.

There was discontent in the ranks and the directors got to hear of this and took some of Livingstone's authority away from him. Naturally, no manager would stand for such interference. Livingstone wanted players who wanted to play for Newcastle United, not prima donnas only interested in a good wage, so he walked out and joined Fulham. It was a very sad situation. Unfortunately, the one player he seemed to have taken his anger out on was Jackie Milburn, whose credentials were impeccable. Milburn was dropped from the side by Livingstone who was then ordered to reinstate him! The question has to be asked: who do directors support, players or their manager? Milburn was close to the end of his United playing career; in fact, he left the club in 1957. Whether we agree or not, Dug Livingstone believed he was doing the right thing and for that he deserves at least some credit.

LORMOR, ANTHONY. A tremendously exciting talent, Lormor began his United career in the 1987-88 season. As a striker, he went on to make six starts, two more as a substitute, and score three goals before a move to Lincoln City. Lormor is now very much a lower-league player. He has certainly proved himself to be an astute goalscorer since he left St James's Park.

LOW, JIMMY. Ex-Glasgow Rangers right-winger Jimmy Low cost United £1,300. A relatively small footballer, just 5′6″ tall, he gave the appearance of being lightweight. In fact, Low was difficult to knock off the ball and would ride tackles as though they had never occurred. He was a marvellous provider of the ball who went on to make 121 appearances and score nine goals in his time at St James's Park, 1921 to 1928.

LOW, WILF. A tall, elegant Scottish international centre-half, Wilf Low was perhaps the best centre-half United have ever had. Powerful and dominant, he marshalled those around him in military fashion. Signed for just £800 in May 1909 and continued to turn out for the first team until 1924. He made a grand total of 367 appearances, scored nine goals, and made a further 11 Wartime League appearances. Low was a remarkable character; he took his football during the game very seriously, yet off the park his quick wit and humour lifted morale and united the team. He made a total of five Scottish international appearances.

LOWERY, JERRY. This goalkeeper, a product of local football, signed professional for United in June 1947. He made six appearances between 1947 and 1952, when he was sold to Lincoln City.

LOWERY, WILLIAM. Tall, thick-set goalkeeper Lowery signed for United from Blyth in 1893 in United's first-ever season in the Football League. The local keeper had previous experience with Gateshead NER and Trafalgar. He made 30 appearances for the club between 1893 and 1895.

LOWRIE, GEORGE. Welsh international inside-forward who signed from Coventry City in March 1948. Lowrie seemed a useful acquisition and in his short spell with the club (until September 1949) he made 12 full appearances and scored five goals. He moved to Bristol City then later back to Coventry City.

LUKE, GEORGE. A product of the United youth team, Luke spent two separate spells at the club. Initially signing professional terms in December 1950 he was released to Hartlepool United in October 1953. After some outstanding performances on the left wing he returned to St James's Park in October 1959 and went on to make 29 appearances and score four goals before he again left the club, signing for Darlington in January 1961.

M

McCAFFREY, AIDEN. Aiden McCaffrey was a local player who signed as an apprentice and turned professional in January 1975, having already obtained England youth international honours. A tall, lanky defender, he made his League debut against Ipswich in 1975 and went on to make 68 appearances, eight more as a substitute, and score five goals for the club. McCaffrey was sold to Derby County in August 1978. From there on in he had a fairly undistinguished career with Bristol Rovers, Bristol City (loan), Torquay (loan), Exeter City, Hartlepool, then finally Carlisle United, firstly as player-coach in 1988 and then as manager in April 1991. Carlisle struggled under his leadership, and McCaffrey was dismissed in September 1992.

McCALL, BILLY. Glaswegian outside-left, Billy McCall was signed from Aberdeen in January 1948. He made 16 appearances and scored four goals during the 1947–48 season.

McCOLL, BOB. As far as centre-forwards went in 1901, it would be hard to find a bigger name than Bob McColl, who signed for United from Queens Park. He was very much a celebrity in his native Scotland; a hat-trick against England in 1901 had ensured his notoriety. Between 1901 and 1904 McColl made 67 appearances and scored 20 goals for the club. He was a real superstar, one of the first to sign for the club.

McCOMBIE, ANDREW. Full-back signed for a then record transfer fee of £700. The moustachioed McCombie *was* Newcastle United. He loved the club very much and remained a player between 1904 and 1910. However, he maintained an involvement at St James's Park until long after the Second World War. A Scottish international, he went on to make 131 appearances for the Magpies, without scoring a solitary goal.

McCRACKEN, WILLIAM. Notorious full-back between 1904 and 1923 McCracken was allegedly signed after an illegal approach from Colin Veitch. Without getting too deeply involved in that side of things, McCracken was a fine addition to the United team. He was instrumental in bringing about a change to the offside rule in 1925 by literally abusing the rules in force at that time. He was renowned all over England as a real battler, as his determination to win every game often spilled over into the realms of recklessness and opponents suffered the effects of his over-enthusiasm. He gained 17 full caps as an Irish international and made 432 appearances for the club, scoring eight goals. During his time at St James's Park he won three Championship medals, an FA Cup-winner's medal and three runners-up medals. He retired from playing in 1922 and went into club management with Hull City, then Gateshead, Millwall and finally Aldershot. He returned to Newcastle as a scout and later moved to Watford. He died in Hull in 1979.

McCREERY, DAVID. A real workhorse in the United midfield, McCreery had a splendid reputation as a player. He made 262 appearances, seven more as a substitute, and scored two goals between 1982 and 1989. The Irish international, with 67 caps, had previously played for Manchester United and Queens Park Rangers among others. After his playing days had ended he turned to club management with Carlisle United, but failed to turn round the Cumbrians poor fortunes which had diminished under another ex-United star, Aiden McCaffrey.

McCURLEY, JOCK. Reserve centre-forward who made 45 appearances and scored eight goals between 1927 and 1930. He was unfortunate not to gain more League experience because of other quality strikers in the United attack.

McDERMIDD, ROBERT. Experienced full-back signed in 1895 for £7.10s! Previous clubs included West End, Burton, Accrington, Renton, Sunderland Albion and he was signed from Dundee Wanderers. He played 64 games and scored twice between 1895 and 1897.

McDERMOTT, TERRY. His career began with Bury at Gigg Lane in October 1969 where he made 83 League appearances and scored eight goals. McDermott was an architect on the field; his sweet passes and long-range shots were admired by several big clubs, including, of course, Newcastle United, for whom he signed in February 1973. In what was to be his first spell with the club, McDermott made 55 League appearances and was an outstanding performer in the United midfield.

In November 1974 he got his dream move to Liverpool – it was a dream move because he hailed from Kirkby. At Anfield he won countless honours and played alongside Kevin Keegan, a partnership which was to survive for many years. McDermott was honoured as Footballer of the Year in 1982, the same year as he returned to Newcastle. He was a major attraction, and supplied Keegan with many of his goals from cleverly crafted midfield moves. McDermott's second spell at the club lasted until 1984. In all, he made 149 appearances and scored 24 goals. He is currently assistant manager at the club. A player of great experience, few could match his list of honours won.

McDONALD, JOHN. Centre-forward who arrived after being transferred from Liverpool. His signing was a desperate attempt to find a regular goalscorer. It failed; he made 42 appearances and scored only six times between 1912 and 1914.

MACDONALD, MALCOLM. Widely known as SuperMac, this well-built centre-forward was idolised by the United fans. On a good day Macdonald was one of the world's best but on an off-day he could be very bad. Signed from Luton Town in July 1969, Macdonald was a strong, tough striker who had scored 49 League goals in 88 appearances for the Hatters. His arrival on Tyneside was greeted with great enthusiasm. In his opening fixture, at home against Liverpool, Macdonald delivered the goods with three cracking goals in front of a packed St James's Park. International recognition with England saw him score five goals in one England game – still a record to this day. One of the most prolific strikers ever to play for the club, SuperMac made 228 appearances and scored 121 goals. His partnership with fellow United striker John Tudor was one of the best in the game.

Much to the anger of the United support, Macdonald was sold to Arsenal in August 1976. He went on to sign for Swedish side Djorgarden before retiring through injury in 1979. He later dabbled in club management with Fulham and Huddersfield Town. Macdonald was an effervescent character, very much his own man. He was often outspoken, which turned opposition fans against him, something which he seemed to relish. Like him or not, Macdonald was one of the all-time greats for Newcastle United.

McDONALD, NEIL. Tall, Wallsend-born midfielder, Neil McDonald was yet another star-find from Wallsend Boys Club. In his first season, 1982–83, he proved himself to be a real asset with a keen eye for goal and a flair for ball-winning. McDonald went on to make 185 first-team outings, 18 more as a substitute, and scored 28 goals. He was sold to Everton in 1988.

McDONALD, THOMAS. Signed in 1921, Tom McDonald was a terrific left-winger who spent ten happy years at St

James's Park. An exciting player, McDonald was a crowd-pleaser especially when he proved to be a capable goalscorer. He won an FA Cup-winners' medal in 1924, and was an influential part of the United line-up; it was his initial shot which created the first goal when United defeated Villa 2–0. McDonald went on to make 367 appearances and score 113 goals. He was a well-respected United star, and one worthy of the highest acclaim.

MacFARLANE, SANDY. Sandy MacFarlane was signed from Airdrie in 1898. A midfield player, he didn't find life at the club to his liking. Perhaps it was because he could not settle, but MacFarlane failed to recreate the kind of performance he had shown in the Scottish game. An international, he made 86 appearances for the club and scored 16 goals between 1898 and 1901 when he returned to Scotland and Dundee.

McFAUL, WILLIE. Willie McFaul who signed for the club in November 1966 from Irish side Linfield made 355 appearances in a nine-year spell as a player. Although well-built, he was remarkably agile and pulled off some of the most remarkable saves ever seen at St James's Park. A twisting, full-length dive was one of his specialities effectively denying some of the world's greatest goalscorers. With six full Irish international caps, McFaul had a successful playing career with his sole English League club, Newcastle United. After his playing days ended he took up an assistant coaching position at the club before becoming manager in September 1985. His managerial reign, however, was not so successful. A great deal was expected from McFaul; the fans demanded success, which he was unable to provide; indeed, when he was sacked in October 1988 the club were second from bottom of the first division! A sad end to a gloriously loyal career.

McGARRY, BILL. Team manager from November 1977 until August 1980, Bill McGarry was brought to the club from a coaching position in Saudi Arabia. Many United fans say that he should have stayed there. McGarry was disappointing as a team manager, which was totally out of line with everything else he had achieved in football. At Newcastle he spent lots of money on seemingly wasteful transfers, as some of the game's 'experienced' players were brought to the club, few of which were of proven quality. United struggled to make any impact under McGarry, who was sacked in August 1980.

McGARRY, RON. Born in Whitehaven, Cumbria, McGarry was first spotted by Workington for his prolific scoring in local football. After a short spell at Borough Park he moved to Bolton Wanderers before arriving at St James's Park in December 1962. McGarry was a regular goalscorer whose record speaks for itself: between 1962 and 1967 he made 129 appearances, three more as a substitute, and scored 46 goals. He later moved to Barrow FC.

McGHEE, MARK. The current manager of Leicester City, McGhee was a keen attacker with real grit and determination. In two separate spells at the club, the first between 1977 and 1979, the second from 1989 until 1991, he made 99 appearances, with 13 further substitute appearances, and scored 36 goals. During the 1980s McGhee had won European and domestic honours with Aberdeen when Alex Ferguson was the club's manager.

McGRATH, JOHN. Stocky centre-half John McGrath joined the club from Bury in a £24,000-plus-player deal, with Bob Stokoe moving in the opposite direction. McGrath was a tough tackler and a fierce battler, a typical centre-half of the era. He made 180 appearances, plus one more as a substitute, and scored two goals in his seven-year spell with United between 1961 and 1968. Later he moved to Southampton and then Brighton. He also became club manager of Port Vale, Chester, Preston and then Halifax. He won one England U-23 cap.

McGUIGAN, JOHN. An inside-forward, McGuigan signed first for Scottish club St Mirren before moving into the English game with Southend United in May 1955. With 35

League goals in 126 appearances, McGuigan was snapped up by United in July 1958. He went on to make 55 appearances and score 17 goals before being sold to Scunthorpe United in January 1962. McGuigan was a tricky, swift-footed player who just lacked that little bit extra to make him into something really special.

McINROY, ALBERT. As fine a goalkeeper as was available in 1929, McInroy joined United from Sunderland and was an England international. Tall and well equipped for the toughest challenge, McInroy was the boss in his penalty-area. He made 160 appearances between 1929 and 1934.

McINTOSH, A. Defender who made 103 appearances and scored two goals between 1920 and 1924.

McKANE, JOSEPH. This ex-Newcastle East End midfielder was signed from Dumbarton. McKane was awesome to look at: short hair, long, thick moustache and a wicked stare. Featured in United's first-ever League fixture, he made a total of 44 appearances between 1891 and 1895.

McKAY, ROBERT. Scored a hat-trick on his United debut versus West Bromwich Albion. Bought from Rangers in a £3,000 transfer deal, McKay was an experienced pro-fessional with skill and technique to match anything in the English game. He made 66 appearances and netted 23 goals between 1926 and 1928. He was also capped by Scotland.

McKAY, WILLIAM. Another striker signed from Rangers, McKay made a total of 21 appearances for United, scoring seven goals between 1895 and 1897.

McKELLAR, DAVID. Goalkeeper who was forced to retire through back injury, McKellar was a large Scot who played just six games for United in 1986 and proved to be reliable enough. Had it not been for his back problem he would have gone on to greater things. The best years of his career were spent at Carlisle United.

McKENZIE, RODERICK. Although originally from Inverness, this United youth talent signed for the club in 1922. A tireless worker in midfield, McKenzie was vociferous and quick-tempered. His tenacity often dominated the midfield as he earned a reputation as a hard-man. He made 256 appearances and scored seven goals between 1922 and 1935.

McKINNEY, WILLIAM. A local-born defender, McKinney signed professional terms in May 1956, making his League debut a short time later. He made 94 appearances and scored eight goals before being sold to Bournemouth in August 1965. He was very much a reserve-team player.

McMENEMY, HARRY. Harry was an inside-forward from Strathclyde Juniors. He made many impressive performances in his 148 appearances and scored 35 goals between 1931 and 1937. His career was unfortunately hampered by countless injuries. He is related to the ex-United star and Sunderland and Southampton manager, Lawrie McMenemy.

McMICHAEL, ALF. McMichael is United's most capped player of all time turning out for his country, Northern Ireland, 40 times. This red-haired left-back became a real leader in the United defence. Signed from Linfield in September 1949, he remained at the club until 1962 and made a total of 431 appearances but scored only one goal.

McNAMEE, JOHN. A terrace idol because of his aggressive attitude on the pitch, McNamee was signed from Hibernian in December 1966. As a centre-half, he was rather cumbersome but lost very few aerial challenges. Made a total of 129 appearances, three more as a substitute, and scored eight goals. McNamee's influence in the heart of the United defence was of paramount importance, especially during the triumphant Fairs Cup campaign of 1969.

McNEE, JOCK. Scottish-born forward signed in 1894 who remained with the club for just one season, making 23 appearances and scoring only once.

McNEIL, MATTHEW. Hibernian centre-half signed by United in December 1949. A rather ordinary player whilst at the club, McNeil made just 11 appearances without a goal before being sold to Barnsley in August 1951.

McWILLIAM, PETER. Allegedly kidnapped by United directors as he was en route to Sunderland for a trial and possible contract, McWilliam joined United in 1902, making his debut against Middlesbrough that same season. He struggled as a half-back in those early days. It was not too long, however, before he was to break back into the first team and there he remained. McWilliam became one of the most consistent performers United have ever had. Rarely having a bad game, he won many honours with the club and a number of Scottish international caps. After 240 appearances and 12 goals, his playing career was ended by a cruel ligament injury. He went on to manage Tottenham Hotspur for 14 years before leaving for Middlesbrough. However, seven years later he left Boro and took on scouting duties for Arsenal. Then, in May 1938, he returned to manage Tottenham for a second spell. His managerial years were as successful as his playing days and he earned an outstanding reputation.

MAHONEY, MIKE. This goalkeeper, who made 135 appearances between 1975 and 1978, began his career at Bristol City before a move to Torquay United in August 1970. He arrived at St James's Park in March 1975 and was a good reflex keeper.

MAITLAND, ALF. Bought from Middlesbrough in 1924, this quick-thinking full-back went on to make 163 appearances for United between 1924 and 1930 and was part of the Championship-winning side of 1927.

MANAGERS. United have had a total of 17 official first-team managers since 1930. Prior to that, the secretary, Frank Watt, ran first-team affairs. Stan Seymour also managed the club twice.

The Newcastle United managers in chronological order are:

Andy Cunningham:	January 1930–May 1935
Tom Mather:	June 1935–September 1939
Stan Seymour:	September 1939–March 1947
George Martin:	May 1947–December 1950
Stan Seymour:	December 1950–December 1954
Dug Livingstone:	December 1954–January 1956
Charlie Mitten:	June 1958–October 1961
Norman Smith:	October 1961–June 1962
Joe Harvey:	June 1962–June 1975
Gordon Lee:	June 1975–February 1977
Richard Dinnis:	February 1977–November 1977
Bill McGarry:	November 1977–August 1980
Arthur Cox:	September 1980–May 1984
Jack Charlton:	May 1984–August 1985
Willie McFaul:	September 1985–October 1988
Jim Smith:	December 1988–March 1991
Ossie Ardiles:	March 1991–February 1992
Kevin Keegan:	February 1992–to date

MARSHALL, GORDON. Ex-Heart of Midlothian keeper signed by the club in June 1963. Marshall, who was very much the boss of his own domain, made 187 appearances between 1963 and 1968.

MARTIN, DENNIS. Tall, slimline winger, Dennis Martin's career started at Kettering Town before a move to West Bromwich Albion, where he continued to improve sufficiently to attract the attention of Carlisle United. He was an integral part of United's Division 1 campaign side of 1974–75. Martin arrived at Newcastle in October 1977, where he played nine games, two more as a substitute, and scored twice, before a move to Mansfield Town in 1978.

MARTIN, GEORGE. Newcastle United manager between 1947 and December 1950. A genuine fellow, Martin achieved promotion for the team during his relatively brief spell at the club, when United finished as Division 2 runners-up in 1948. This success was followed by a solid season back in the top flight when the team finished fourth. In December 1950 he moved to Aston Villa. A proud man,

128

he also had a good playing career with clubs such as Hull City, Everton, Middlesbrough and Luton Town.

MARTIN, MICK. Much-travelled midfielder who arrived via Manchester United and West Bromwich Albion before signing for United in December 1978. Martin made 155 appearances, eight more as a substitute, and scored six goals.

MATHER, THOMAS. United manager between June 1935 and September 1939. Although he had never made a career *playing* football, Mather had a great deal of experience in football-club administration. His time at United followed spells with Manchester City, Bolton Wanderers, Southend and Stoke City. As a manager, Mather achieved very little at St James's Park and he left Newcastle when war broke out.

MATHIE, ALEX. Signed from Scottish club side Morton for a fee of £250,000 in July 1993. A forward, Mathie failed to make a first-team place his own, and, apart from a spectacular goal against Sheffield Wednesday, was less than inspiring. Despite this, manager Kevin Keegan doubled the player's transfer fee when he was sold to Ipswich Town in February 1995.

MATHISON, GEORGE. Locally-born wing-half, George Mathison hailed from Walker. His uninspiring performances ensured that he played mainly reserve-team football. Mathison did make 22 first-team outings between 1926 and 1933 but never quite lived up to everyone's expectations.

MEGSON, GARY. Tall, red-haired midfielder, Megson was a very influential player on the pitch. Signed in 1984 from Nottingham Forest, he had previously played for Plymouth, Everton and Sheffield Wednesday. Injuries kept him out of the United line-up, though he did make 24 outings, four more as a substitute, and scored two goals between 1984 and 1986, when he returned to Wednesday.

MELLOR, WILLIAM. Goalkeeper Mellor, signed as cover for Jimmy Lawrence, never quite matched his predecessor. In one game, at White Hart Lane, he managed to injure himself in the pre-match kick-about, taking himself out of the game! He made 25 appearances between 1914 and 1920.

MILBURN, JOHN. Also known as 'Wor Jackie', Milburn was the most idolised player yet to don a black-and-white shirt. John Edward Thompson Milburn made 397 first-class appearances for United and bagged some 200 goals between 1943 and 1957. Exciting, innovative and downright arrogant with a ball at his feet, Jackie Milburn was pure genius. A Wembley FA Cup-winner (twice), he had a flair which has yet to be matched in modern-day football. His England full international appearances were limited to just 13, but nine goals were netted for his country.

In 1957 he went into club management with Linfield, who offered him a lucrative contract. During his spell in Ireland he continued to play and was voted Ulster Footballer of the Year in 1958, the same year that Linfield were runners-up in the Irish Cup. Milburn led them to eventual Cup success in 1960.

November 1960 saw him take over as player-manager of Yiewsley, where he remained for two years. Following this, there was a brief coaching role in Reading, then on to Ashington, before he took the helm at Ipswich Town in January 1963. Milburn made few mistakes as a player, but accepting the job of manager was one of the worst moves he made. Town were on a downward spiral with a poor side and no funds. The club were to be relegated in 1964 and Jackie stayed for a few more months, until September 1963 when he finally came home to manage Gateshead. He later took up a career in sports journalism in the North East. The master passed away on 9 October 1988 and to this day his name is synonymous with that of Newcastle United. I feel sure it will remain so.

MILLER, WILLIAM. Signed from Scottish club Kilmarnock in 1895, Miller played 48 times and scored twice for Newcastle between 1895 and 1897. Unfortunately, he is remembered for a two-week club suspension for his alleged part in the theft of two rings in 1895. It is not for us to discuss his guilt here, but the club certainly took a dim view of his character thereafter.

MILLS, DAVID. Whitby-born striker David Mills is best remembered by the average fan as a Middlesbrough player. However, after a lengthy spell at Ayresome Park, he joined West Bromwich Albion and then signed on loan for United in January 1982. However, 23 League games and four goals later, he was off to Sheffield Wednesday, before returning to St James's Park on a more permanent basis in August 1983. Sadly Mills had little to offer the club by this stage in his career. Although well experienced and an undoubted goalscorer, he had lost his pace and the youthful petulance which used to excite the fans. He made 16 more League appearances and scored nine goals before moving back to Middlesbrough.

MIRANDINHA, FRANCISCO. 'Mira' was everyone's darling, a much-needed terrace hero at the time. Standing at only 5'8" in his stocking feet, Mira was hardly a target man, though he did possess a terrific shot and could turn on a sixpence. Signed for £575,000 from Fluminese, he announced at his first press conference, that 'I want to score goals for Newcastle United'. He did, netting 23 in 55 appearances between 1987 and 1990. Sadly, Mira's desire to win was not as great as those around him. Yes, he was a genius with the ball at his feet, but an all-too-expensive one. Mira was no ball-winner, and for long periods in some games he would virtually disappear. Quite often the rest of the side carried him until, of course, a goal-scoring opportunity came his way – then Mira would do his stuff. Unfortunately in a struggling side, goalscoring chances are few and the Brazilian quietly slipped out of the English game.

MITCHELL, KENNETH. Mitchell was a defender who signed for the club as an apprentice, turning professional in April 1975. Between 1976 and 1980 he made 66 appearances, plus six more as a substitute, and scored two

Francisco Mirandinha

goals. He never quite established himself as a regular first-teamer, and signed for Darlington in August 1981.

MITCHELL, ROBERT. Arguably the greatest outside-left United have ever had was signed from Third Lanark for £16,000 in February 1949. Bobby Mitchell was a revelation. His mazy runs down the left flank with the ball seemingly attached to his left boot were a pleasure to behold. Capped twice by Scotland, he made the best decision of his life in moving to Tyneside. He was an integral part of the successful United line-up of the 1950s. An FA Cup-winner twice, he netted the second United goal in the 3–1 victory over Manchester City in the 1955 final. This was a well-executed shot from an acute angle which left Trautmann in the City goal grasping at fresh air as the ball flashed past him, low and hard like a Scud missile. In 408 games Bobby Mitchell went on to score 113 goals. He almost signed for Notts County in the late 1950s but failed to agree terms and remained at St James's Park until 1961 when he joined Berwick Rangers. Bobby had a heart as big as Newcastle itself, never ever giving up on a seemingly lost cause. His outstanding contribution won many fixtures for the club. Bobby Mitchell is yet another United all-time great!

MITCHELL, STEWART. Between 1953 and 1963, this reserve-team keeper had great difficulty in ousting United's first-choice keeper, Ronnie Simpson. A Glaswegian, Mitchell made just 48 first-team outings in his ten-year spell at the club.

MITTEN, CHARLES. Newcastle United manager between June 1958 and October 1961. Largely unsuccessful in his reign at the club, Mitten's side were, at best, average. His first full season saw the club exit from the FA Cup in an ignominious 4–1 home defeat in the third round and wallow in mid-table obscurity in Division 1. The following season saw little improvement. In 1961 the side were finally relegated from Division 1, finishing second-bottom with just 32 points, having suffered 21 League defeats. After this, it came as no surprise when Mitten was sacked by the United board.

MITTEN, JOHN. This winger, signed from Mansfield Town in September 1960, is the son of ex-United manager Charlie Mitten. John Mitten excelled at all sports and was a first-class cricketer with Leicestershire. At United he was limited to just ten first-team outings and scored three goals before being transferred to Leicester City in September 1961; he later moved to Manchester United, Coventry City, Plymouth and finally Exeter City.

MONCUR, ROBERT. Scottish-born centre-half Moncur was a player of outstanding class who went on to represent his country at Schoolboy, U-23, and full international levels. Signed professional terms with United in April 1962 and remained with the club until June 1974. The young Moncur soon established himself as a hard and effective central defender. His three-goal contribution won United the 1969 Fairs Cup. The pick of the bunch came from an exhilarating burst through the left midfield, a quick one-two with Ben Arentoft and then *crack* – the ball flew into Ujpesti's net. Between 1960 and 1974, Moncur made 343 appearances, three more as a substitute, and scored eight goals. He signed for Sunderland in June '74 and remained there until November 1976, when he took the managerial reins at Carlisle United. He failed to inspire the struggling Cumbrians but did discover Peter Beardsley, signing him for the cost of a set of playing shirts! His managerial days were less distinguished than his playing ones and he drifted from Carlisle to Hearts to Plymouth and then Hartlepool United via Whitley Bay.

MONKHOUSE, ALAN. Centre-forward signed from Millwall in October 1953, Monkhouse was effectively returning home. A Stockton lad, he had high hopes of proving himself at St James's Park. In 21 appearances he scored nine goals but somehow failed to inspire. He was sold to York City in June 1956.

MOONEY, EDWARD. Mooney was a solid, fresh-faced wing-half who joined from Walker Celtic. An uncompromising player, he gave 100 per cent every game. Between 1919 and 1927 he made 135 appearances and scored four goals.

MOONEY, THOMAS. This forward made 80 first-team appearances and scored 19 goals in his war-disrupted period at the club between 1936 and 1944.

MORRIS, PETER. Already respected as a player with Mansfield, Ipswich and then Norwich, Morris arrived at St

James's Park after a managerial spell with Mansfield Town, where the club won the Division 4 Championship under his guidance. He was assistant manager to Bill McGarry at United between February 1978 and February 1979. Many felt that Morris would have been a better manager than McGarry. He moved to become manager at Peterborough, Crewe, Southend, Kettering Town, and then Boston United, until he took over as assistant manager at Northampton Town in 1994.

MORTENSEN, STANLEY. Yes, this legendary figure did actually don the United black-and-white shirt. Sadly it was in a Wartime League game when Mort was but 21 years of age! He later signed professional terms for Blackpool.

MULGREW, THOMAS. Signed from Northampton Town in October 1952, Mulgrew was an inside-forward who had impressed United scouts in his time at the County Ground. He made 14 appearances and scored one goal for United before being transferred to Southampton in July 1954, where he was a prolific scorer with 91 goals from 293 League appearances. He went on to play for Aldershot.

MURRAY, JAMES. A utility player, signed by Andy Cunningham from Glasgow Rangers, Murray was a gifted footballer who could fill any role required of him. With superb ball-skills and a great ability to read the game, he became a popular member of the United line-up between 1932 and 1936. He made 96 appearances and scored ten goals.

MUTCH, ANDREW. Sandy Mutch was a well-travelled and experienced goalkeeper when he signed for United in 1922. He was, in fact, 38 years of age and he had had a notable career at Leeds Road with Huddersfield Town. He made 43 appearances between 1922 and 1924. The Mutch family association does not end there; Sandy was later part of the groundstaff at St James's Park and his son, Alec, was later to become part of the backroom staff.

NATRASS, IRVING. A rapid rise through United's junior ranks saw this Fishburn-born youngster establish himself as a fine defender and break into United's first team. Natrass signed professional terms in July 1970. A solidly built player, he was often found in the opponent's penalty-box and had as sweet a shot as any forward. This attacking flair saw him hit 20 goals in a total of 275 appearances, with a further 12 games as a substitute. He earned a solitary cap for England at U-23 level. In August 1979 Natrass signed for Middlesbrough where he went on to make over 140 appearances.

NAYLOR, JIMMY. Half-back signed from Huddersfield Town for a fee of £4,000. Jimmy Naylor had been impressive for the Yorkshire side and the United manager, Andy Cunningham, believed that the player would be a great influence at St James's Park. He wasn't, for like several other players it seems that he could not live up to everyone's expectations once wearing the black-and-white striped shirt. Naylor lasted just two years, making 32 appearances, before moving to Oldham.

NEALE, DUNCAN. Born in Worthing, Sussex, Duncan Neale was signed from non-League side Ilford in June 1959.

A wing-half, he arrived at St James's Park and was excited about his move to the North East. There were no doubts about his tenacity nor his skill. Neale was unfortunate because there were so many other quality players pushing for his position. Eventually it all became too much for him and, after playing 98 games and scoring 12 goals, he was sold to Plymouth Argyle in August 1963. This was a great shame as he could no doubt have become a very high-profile footballer had he believed in himself a little more.

NEILSON, ALAN. Neilson is a German-born Welsh international full-back who wrote to the club requesting a trial and duly received one. He is currently playing much of his football in the United reserves but Kevin Keegan has already seen enough to confirm that the defender has a good future ahead of him. He may well have to wait for his opportunity, though, such is the calibre of the current United defence.

NELSON, JIMMY. Jimmy Nelson was a Scottish international full-back who arrived in a £7,000 transfer deal from Cardiff City in 1930. At the age of 30 many people questioned the relatively high transfer fee, but Nelson soon proved his doubters wrong. He was impressive as a team leader and went on to captain United to their 1932 Wembley triumph. He made 159 appearances without a single goal although his influence was far greater than this suggests.

NIBLO, THOMAS. Scottish international winger who was with United for two separate spells, 1898–1902 and 1907–8. In between, Niblo had spent some time with Aston Villa with whom he gained an outstanding reputation. He made a career total of 60 appearances for United and scored five goals.

NICHOLSON, GARY. Newcastle-born attacker who graduated through the junior ranks to break into the United first team. Signed professional in November 1978, he made just 11 appearances, five more as a substitute, without making a particularly crucial impact. A youngster who had loads of potential, it became obvious that he would stand a greater chance of success of first-team football with a different club. So, in August 1981, he joined Mansfield Town where his career blossomed, albeit in the lower divisions.

NICKNAME. The nickname 'Magpies' has been attributed to a number of sources, all from around 1895. The following are just three of the most popular theories. A Dominican priest, Father Dalamatius Houtmann, a Dutchman resident at Blackfriars Monastery, Newcastle, was a keen United fan and because he was always dressed in black and white he was identified as having the appearance of a magpie. He was forever at the ground mixing with club officials.

Another favourite, which is perhaps more accurate, is quite simply that the new club colours, which had been instated in August 1894, matched the black and white plumage of the magpie bird and so the team became known as the Magpies.

Finally, there was some suggestion that a pair of magpies were perennially nesting in the main stand at St James's Park.

NOBLE, PETER. A midfielder whose quality was realised elsewhere, Peter Noble signed as an apprentice before turning professional in April 1967. His 22 appearances (three more as substitute) and seven goals were all he mustered at St James's Park before he moved to Swindon Town. His balding head, complete with combed-over 'Bobby Charlton' style strands of hair made him stand out from the crowd. Noble was a real character and a native of Newcastle whose ball-winning tenacity and passing ability allowed him to excel. Although he also played for Burnley and Blackpool, he remained at Newcastle between 1964 (as an apprentice) until January 1968.

NON-LEAGUE OPPOSITION. All these games were played as Newcastle United FC. Apart from the FA Cup qualifying rounds of 1895–96 and 1897–98, United have actually met non-League opposition in first-class fixtures (FA Cup) on 19 occasions. These do not include fixtures against Division 3 N/S sides. Of these 19, some 13 have been won. The six defeats listed chronologically are:-

1892/93 Middlesbrough 3–2 FAC 1.
1897/98 Southampton St Mary's 1–0 FAC 2.
1899/1900 Southampton 4–1 FAC 2. First game abandoned at 0–0.
1906/07 Crystal Palace 1–0 FAC 1.
1963/64 Bedford Town 2–1 FAC 3.
1971/72 Hereford United 2–1 FAC 3 after 2–2 draw at St James's.

This is not exactly the poor non-league cup record the club have been accused of. With the exception of Bedford Town, all are now members of the football league! So the non-League opposition jinx is quite simply historically inaccurate. The last non-League team to face United in a first class fixture was Hendon of the Isthmian League in the FA Cup third round in 1973/74; after a 1–1 draw at home, United won 4–0 at Vicarage Road, Watford.

NULTY, GEOFF. Nulty was an industrious, often over-zealous midfielder, a real tiger in the heart of the United team. His career began with Stoke City, before a move to Burnley in July 1968. United signed him in December 1974 and he went on to make 123 appearances and score 14 goals. Nulty's stamina was incredible; a 90-minute man, he would hustle and bustle the opposition into making mistakes. He was sold to Everton in July 1978.

O

OATES, GRAHAM. Yorkshireman whose playing career began with Bradford City in February 1970. As a midfielder he shone in the Division 3 Bantams side. Blackburn Rovers were next to notice his promise and duly signed him in 1974. Oates eventually arrived at Newcastle in March 1976 but found it difficult to break into the first team. Eventually he made just 29 appearances, nine more as a substitute, and scored three goals.

OLDEST CUP-FINAL PLAYER. William Hampson was 41 years and eight months old when he appeared in the 1924 FA Cup final for United, the oldest player to appear in such a final.

OLDEST DEBUT. Andy Cunningham was 38 years and three days old when he made his debut for United in February 1929. Within 11 months of doing so, he had became the club's first-ever official manager.

O'BRIEN, LIAM. Influential, skilful international midfielder signed from Manchester United in 1988. O'Brien had two cultured feet and his eye for a long-range accurate pass was incredible, as was his will to win. O'Brien went on to make

152 appearances and score 21 goals, with 22 appearances as a substitute. He was sold to Tranmere Rovers for a fee of £250,000 in January 1994. Although often injury-prone, he ran the United midfield during a difficult rebuilding programme. The majority of his 21 goals were spectacular rather than ordinary and will remain with fans as testimony to his shooting prowess.

O'NEILL, LES. Diminutive midfielder who unfortunately slipped through the club's net. O'Neill was a lively character who was signed from Blyth Spartans in November 1961. Amazingly, he made just one appearance for the club before moving on to Darlington. It was much later in his career, around 1974–75, that O'Neill came to the fore with Carlisle United, when he scored one of the most sensational goals ever seen on BBC TV's *Match of the Day*, as Carlisle made a grand entrance into Division 1 football. O'Neill might have proved to be a great asset for United, but such was the quantity and quality of players emerging through local-league football that it was inevitable that some would be lost – Les O'Neill was one such player.

O'NEILL, MICHAEL. Skilful forward who was signed in 1987 from Coleraine, in Northern Ireland. O'Neill made 41 appearances and scored 16 goals between 1987 and 1989 when he was sold to Dundee United FC. His first Newcastle goal was netted in a 3–1 away victory over Oxford United in December 1987, though his greatest performance in a United shirt was at St James's Park when he netted a hat-trick against Luton Town on 2 April 1988. He now plays for Hibernian, where he has continued to play some superb football and score a number of spectacular goals.

ORR, RONALD. A striker who came from St Mirren in May 1901, Ronald Orr gave the appearance of being too small for a professional footballer, standing at just 5'5", but he once scored four goals in a game against Notts County which made him an instant favourite with the crowd. Favouritism, however, can quickly diminish when players upset fans – and Ronald Orr certainly upset the loyal stalwarts at United. It seems unlikely that we will ever know what really happened but it is claimed he screamed abuse at a certain section of the crowd after having been criticised for his standard of play. It was a great shame as Orr was a fine player; scoring 69 goals in 180 appearances, between 1901 and 1908, is a good record. His goals helped United win the Championship in 1905 and 1907.

OSTLER, JACK. Tall, lean centre-half who signed from Motherwell in 1896 for a fee of £200, which incorporated a further signing by the club. Ostler was a law unto himself: he readily voiced his opinions and was not a man to mince his words. On the pitch he was equally as honest and gave his all. Between 1896 and 1900 he made 74 appearances and scored three goals.

P

PAPAVASILIOU, NIKI. Small, creative midfielder signed from OFI Iraklion in July 1993 for a fee of £125,000. Niki is a left-footed player with a spendid touch. A Cypriot international, he is a handy player to have available and has been more than a little unfortunate not to hold down a first-team place. When he was first signed, his surname caused horrendous problems for the United terrace chant as very little rhymes with it. This problem was solved by simply constantly repeating it!

PARK, JOHN. Centre-forward from Hamilton Academical, John Park was seen as the answer to United's goal famine of 1936. A large, well-built player, Park had a difficult time at Newcastle: his bustling style was lost in the English game and he scored just 12 goals in 61 appearances, between 1936 and 1940.

PARK, OSSIE. Ossie was a powerful centre-half, signed from Darlington in 1924 who went on to make 43 appearances for the club. He was something of an expert at filling in for players hit by injury. He played four games in United's Championship-winning season of 1926–27.

PATERSON, WILLIAM. W.A.K. Paterson's professional football career began with Doncaster Rovers in 1950. At Belle Vue he had made 113 League appearances as centre-half before signing for Newcastle in October 1954. A Scottish 'B' international, he struggled at St James's Park and made just 22 appearances, scoring only one goal between 1954 and 1957.

PAYNE, LEE. Payne, signed from Barnet in 1988, and made his full United debut against Middlesbrough in October 1988 in a 3–0 victory. Payne operated from the left-wing but never quite provided the flair United required. He made six full appearances, one more as a substitute, before moving on to Reading FC later that same season, 1988–89.

PEACOCK, DARREN. The tall, slim central-defender Darren Peacock is an unmistakable giant in the present United team. His long flowing locks are as much part of his image as his heading power. Peacock likes nothing more than a sortie into the opposition-box, although he never really makes his presence felt by converting aerial chances into goals. He initially played for Newport County before moving to Hereford United and then to Queens Park Rangers. He cost the club £2,700,000 when they brought him from Loftus Road in March 1994. There are few better central-defenders in the Premier League today.

PEACOCK, GAVIN. Ex-Queens Park Rangers, Gillingham and Bournemouth striker who arrived at St James's in the 1990–91 season. The slim-built Peacock was an outstanding striker who had everything – pace, touch and that decisive killer-instinct in front of goal. He was idolised by the United faithful and is still greatly respected. Peacock's honesty and determination make him one of the country's great strikers but he seems confused by media attention and so is often underestimated. Peacock moved to London and Chelsea in the 1993–94 season for personal reasons which were unrelated to Newcastle United or the fans. He is a tremendous player who will score goals wherever he plays.

Gavin Peacock

PEARSON, JAMES. Scottish U-23 international midfielder who greatly disappointed during his term at the club – Pearson had the ability but lacked the determination. He was signed by Everton from Scottish side St Johnstone in July 1974 and arrived at St James's Park in August 1978, making 11 appearances and scoring three goals in the 1978–79 season. Pearson was hardly the type of cultured midfielder United fans had been used to. In the end, injury wrecked his career.

147

PEARSON, THOMAS. Pearson has the unusual distinction of being capped by both Scotland and England. This tricky forward, a Scot by birth, was capped by England during the war. He came to Newcastle as a youngster from Murrayfield Amateurs. A master of the dribble, he could send defenders one way then the other by a simple drop of the shoulder. He made 228 appearances and scored 52 goals between 1933 and 1948.

PEART, JACK. An experienced striker signed from Stoke City at the begnning of the 1912–13 season, Peart flattered to deceive in his one season at the club, although his record elsewhere was reasonably good. He made 17 appearances and scored six goals before being released at the end of that season.

PEDDIE, JOCK. A goalscoring hero who was signed from Third Lanark for £135 in 1897. Peddie was, to put it mildly, dynamite! He would often pick up the ball and set off on a run from the halfway line before launching a thunderbolt-like shot towards the opposition goal. He disliked conforming to rules and regulations and was very much his own man, which endeared him to the hearts of the Tyneside following. United have never really had a centre-forward like him since then and he is something of a legend at St James's Park. Peddie made 135 appearances and scored 78 goals. Today his value would far exceed that paid for Andy Cole. One fan described him as 'a striker's striker' – which sums him up.

PENALTIES. United have been involved in a number of dramatic penalty situations. The worst was in 1958 when, in three consecutive fixtures, penalties were awarded the club's way. Incredibly Allchurch, White and the 17-year-old John Mitten all missed. The boot was on the other foot when, during a fixture with Manchester City on 27 December 1912, United conceded three penalties! All of these were duly missed by the City players (Fletcher 2, Thornley 1) and the game ended in a 1–1 draw.

PENMAN, WILLIAM. Glasgow Rangers forward who signed in April 1963, Penman was an articulate footballer. His ball-control was neat and often mazy as he shimmied left then right to deceive defenders. He made a total of 62 appearances and scored 18 goals before being sold to Swindon Town in September 1966. Penman later moved to Walsall in August 1970.

PHILLIPSON, THOMAS. Ex-schoolboy international Thomas Phillipson made a name for himself with the mighty Wolverhampton Wanderers where he netted over 110 goals. He fared reasonly well in Newcastle but never truly settled; in 15 first-team appearances he scored only four goals. Phillipson later moved into local government and was elected mayor of Wolverhampton!

PINGEL, FRANK. Striker signed from FC Aarhus in 1988. Pingel was yet another overseas player who never really settled into the British game. His only goal came in a home game against Liverpool in February 1989 which ended in a 2–2 draw. United's other goal that day was scored by another overseas player who struggled in England, Mirandinha. Pingel remained at St James's Park for just one season and made a total of 13 appearances with one more as a substitute.

PITCH MEASUREMENTS. The approximate perimeter measurements of the pitch at St James's Park are 115 yards x 75 yards.

PRIOR, GEORGE. Outside-left who had two separate spells with United. During the first, when he was signed from Sunderland Amateurs in March 1952, he made eight appearances until May 1954 when he was sold to Millwall. He scored three goals during this term. Prior later returned in July 1956 but made just two further first-team starts.

PUDAN, DICK. Defender/left-back signed from Bristol Rovers for a fee of £150. Pudan was really a frustrated midfielder and would often stray forward using his deft

149

touch to string together neat passing movements. A thinking player, he was well respected by his peers, many of whom claimed he was the best left-back of his era. Dick Pudan made 30 appearances without scoring between 1906 and 1909.

PUNTON, WILLIE. Born in Perth and first signed by Irish club side Portadown, Willie Punton was transferred to Newcastle in February 1954. Sadly, his initial skill and determination seemed to flounder when he found himself playing reserve-team football. After 23 appearances and only one goal between 1953 and 1957, he was released first to Southend United and then to Norwich, where his career finally took off. He later played for Sheffield United and Scunthorpe.

PYKE, GEORGE. George Pyke was more a reserve centre-forward than regular first-teamer during a Newcastle career which lasted from 1913 until 1922. Although he had the capability to score plenty of goals, he never seemed to deliver the goods in a competitive match. He made 13 appearances and scored three times for United, but his career was sorely interrupted by the war.

Q

QUINN, CHARLES. Striker used in the club's early days whose virtually shaven head apart from a small tuft at the front and small frame gave him an adolescent appearance. He scored five goals from 23 appearances between 1893 and 1896.

QUINN, MICHAEL. Affectionately known as 'Sumo', Quinn was, and still is, a thick-set, well-built striker with a marvellous sense of humour. That part of his character aside, he is also a terrific goalscorer. Naturally talented, he often scored goals from unbelievable positions. Previously on the books of Wigan Athletic, Stockport County, Oldham and Portsmouth, he joined United in 1989 and bagged four goals on his debut against Leeds United at St James's Park. A well-respected player who always received a warm welcome from United fans, Quinn made 126 appearances, seven more as a substitute, and scored 65 goals. He was sold to Coventry in 1993.

R

RAFFERTY, BILLY. Billy Rafferty was a goalscorer whose career had taken him through five clubs prior to arriving at Newcastle, so he was hardly a novice. Although somewhat slow, his main asset was his strength. He made 37 appearances and scored eight goals between October 1979 and December 1980, when he signed for Portsmouth. Rafferty also played five games as a substitute.

RAMSEY, ALEX. This young midfielder broke into the first team for 37 appearances between 1919 and 1921 and scored two goals. He was originally signed from local side Swalwell FC.

RANDALL, CHARLES. Inside-forward who hailed from Burnopfield, but who never projected himself enough to claim a regular first-team place. He scored six goals from 19 appearances between 1908 and 1911.

RANSOM, RAYMOND. Raymond Ransom was a defender who had considerable experience when he arrived at Newcastle in 1988. A determined character, he was an excellent passer of the ball who never gave up a chase. He made a total of 92 appearances, five more as a substitute, and scored once. He was sold back to Manchester City in 1993.

REID, ALEX. Another one-season wonder, Reid arrived from Dundee United in October 1971. Between 1971 and 1973 he made 15 appearances, ten more as a substitute, without scoring a single goal.

REILLY, GEORGE. A tall, gangly striker, Reilly arrived at St James's Park in 1984. He was used to acting as a target-man, but this was not in keeping with United's style of play. Despite doing his best to win over the Newcastle support, he seemed to struggle on the pitch, yet 33 appearances and ten goals is no mean achievement. United supporters remember him with great affection, more for his commitment than for his skill. He moved to West Bromwich Albion in season 1984–85.

RENDELL, THOMAS. A forward who played just one season for United, 1894–95, made 25 appearances and scored two goals. He was another player who arrived as an experimental signing but failed to make the grade on Tyneside.

REPLAYS. In the 1923–24 season United faced Derby County in an FA Cup second-round tie at the Baseball Ground. The game ended 2–2 so a replay was required at St James's Park. This match took place on 6 February 1924, and, after extra-time, again finished 2–2. A second replay was necessary, this time at Bolton Wanderers' Burnden Park ground on 11 February. Incredibly, yet again, the game ended 2–2 after extra-time. A third replay took place after the toss of a coin dictated that United could stage it at St James's Park. This time United won through 5–3. Incidentally, they went on to win the Cup that same year without needing to replay any more matches! Curiously, in the 1931–32 season United needed a replay to defeat Blackpool in the third round, and two replays to see off the challenge of Southport in the fourth round! Again they went on to win the Cup. In 1904–5 two replays were necessary to beat Plymouth Argyle and United went on to reach the final, only to lose to Aston Villa at Crystal Palace's ground. Three replays were required in the 1988–89 competition when Watford eventually ran out 1–0 winners at Vicarage Road.

RICHARDSON, JAMES. Ashington-born inside-forward who spent two spells at the club, 1928–34 and 1937–38. In between, he played for Huddersfield Town. At St James's Park he made 163 appearances and scored 53 goals, and after the war he played for Millwall and Orient. Richardson was also capped by England twice, and represented the Football League as well as England Schools.

RICHARDSON, JOSEPH. This defender, transferred from Blyth Spartans in 1929, was an inspirational signing. Richardson was a solid, reliable defender, who made an art of doing the simple things right. Between 1929 and 1945 he made 223 appearances and scored once.

RIDLEY, JOHN. Reserve-team striker who was signed from Willington Athletic. Ridley made 17 outings and scored twice in his time at the club, between 1907 and 1911.

ROBERTS, RICHARD. Speedy winger with a real flair for going it alone. Roberts' dashing runs down the flanks excited the St James's Park crowds. Signed from West Bromwich Albion in 1901, he was surprisingly sold to Middlesbrough in 1904. There was a great deal of commotion about the move when fans voiced their anger at the club for selling one of its best players to a local rival. Roberts made 55 appearances and scored 17 goals for Newcastle.

ROBINSON, MARK. Midfielder signed from Barnsley in the 1992–93 season. Robinson looked a fair bet for a regular first-team place but was sold to Swindon Town in July 1994 for £600,000, having made just 15 outings, with a further 11 on the substitute bench.

ROBINSON, RAYMOND. Signed from Scotswood, Ray Robinson was a midfielder-cum-striker who notched up four goals from 29 appearances for the club. He was one of several players at the time (1919–20) who never quite made it at Newcastle.

ROBINSON, STUART. This apprentice signed professional in July 1977, made 13 first-team outings, one as a substitute and scored three goals – a reasonable record for the youngster. His attacking flair was utilised for lengthy spells in the reserve line-up, from where Aldershot signed him in July 1980.

ROBLEDO, GEORGE. Born on 14 April 1926 in Chile, George Robledo was 20 and living in England when he signed professional terms for Barnsley. He had previously been playing for Huddersfield Town as an amateur. He made 104 League appearances at Oakwell and scored an incredible 44 goals, which naturally attracted the attention of many of the country's bigger clubs, including Newcastle United. Robledo signed for the Magpies in January 1949 and progressed to become a Chilean international. A real wizard with a football, he was also a tactical schemer who tended to organise his attacking colleagues. Robledo's goal return for United was perhaps one of the greatest: 91 from 164 matches. George was most influential in the signing of Ted Robledo, his older brother – it was a 'take us or leave me' ultimatum. United had no option, so signed both brothers.

George scored the winning goal in the 1952 FA Cup-final victory over Arsenal and also achieved a winners' medal from the previous season's competition. In that same 1951–52 season he equalled Hughie Gallacher's League and Cup scoring record of 39 goals. Robledo was a real star and was fortunate enough to play alongside Jackie Milburn – both were without doubt feeding off each other. Few striking partnerships were as successful as this pair's was, because both men were hungry for goals. It has to be said, though, that Robledo was perhaps the more underestimated of the two.

ROBLEDO, TED. Wing-half and brother of United favourite George Robledo. He signed for Barnsley and made five League appearances for the Tykes in the 1947–48 season and then signed for Newcastle in February 1949, shortly after his brother had done so. Ted was never quite as artistic a player as his younger brother, but he did manage to turn in some fine performances for the club between 1949 and 1953. He made 45 appearances without a goal.

ROBSON, BRYAN. Pop Robson was born in Sunderland and signed for United in November 1962. Although hardly the tallest striker Newcastle have ever had, Robson was certainly one of the most lethal. He would throw himself at crosses, mis-hit shots or anything from which he could possibly score a goal. An opportunist forward, he could pop up when one least expected. As a ball-winner he was fiery and as a distributor he was an expert. He had just about everything and, like his famous namesake was at Manchester United, there can be no denying that Robson was a United idol during his eight years at St James's Park. As well as being a Fairs Cup winner, England U-23 international honours were bestowed upon him as he thrashed in 97 goals in 243 appearances, plus one game as a substitute.

Robson left United in February 1971 for West Ham where he continued to score sensational goals. He later moved to Sunderland (three times in all) Carlisle (twice) West Ham (again) and then Chelsea. He took over as manager of Carlisle United for a short time but left after only a few weeks in office. Robson was a great motivator on the field, which makes his lack of success as a manager something of a mystery.

ROBSON, KEITH. Another local talent, and another striker, Keith Robson was very different to 'Pop' (see above). Signed from the juniors in May 1971, Keith made 15 appearances for the club, scoring five goals. He was a tall, almost stiff-looking, forward, but he had a raw talent which made him a winner. In September 1974 he moved to West Ham and later had spells with Cardiff, Norwich, Leicester and Carlisle.

Bryan 'Pop' Robson

ROBSON, THOMAS. Throughout his career, which started at Northampton Town in August 1961, Robson was an old-fashioned winger – head down and run along the wing. In 1965 he signed for Chelsea before moving back to his home town of Newcastle in December 1966. At St James's Park he found life tough. The quality of the playing staff was high and Robson could never quite claim a regular place in the first team. He made 48 appearances, with two others as a substitute, and scored 11 goals before transferring to Peterborough United in November 1968.

ROCHE, DAVID. Something of a utility player, Roche made his debut as a substitute at Arsenal in 1989. He went on to make 26 starts and 13 substitute appearances, without scoring a goal. Roche had a great deal of promise but, like so many players of his kind, had to move away from United to fulfil his long-term ambitions. He signed for Doncaster Rovers in October 1993 for £25,000.

ROEDER, GLENN. This astute, experienced defender provided some excellent service to the club. Roeder had started his playing career at Orient, then moved to Queens Park Rangers, before a brief loan spell at Notts County and an eventual transfer to Newcastle in 1983. A team leader, he was committed to his game and on the field had something of a dour personality. This was largely due to the concentration he put into every touch, every move, every thought. Roeder pushed his colleagues all the way. He made 215 appearances and scored ten goals between 1983 and 1988 and was a player of such quality that it made him difficult to replace. He later moved to Watford, Orient and Gillingham, where he had a spell as manager before taking over at Watford.

ROGERS, EHUD. Right-winger of the old school, Rogers was a Welsh amateur international whilst with Oswestry Town. He later signed for Wrexham and Arsenal, before arriving at St James's Park in 1936. An elegant player, he was tricky on the ball and could provide good crosses, supplying his fellow forwards with plenty of ammunition. Between 1936 and 1939 he made 58 appearances and scored ten goals. He returned to Wrexham after the war.

ROGERS, JOSEPH. Signed from Grimsby Town in 1898, Rogers was a prolific goalscorer, and once scored five times in an FA representative game. Rogers was vastly experienced by the time of his arrival at Newcastle, which served his colleagues well. He made 54 appearances and scored 11 goals.

ROGERS, THOMAS. Left-back signed from Scottish side St Johnstone in 1892. He made just 24 appearances for

United. Unlike many of his contemporaries who found the transition between the style of football in Scotland and England relatively easy, Rogers failed to achieve the standards he had set himself in Scotland.

ROXBURGH, ROBERT. Another local talent who made more of a name for himself away from St James's Park. A defender, Roxburgh was spotted by local scouts and signed for the club in 1920. However, a series of indifferent performances meant that he could hardly justify a first-team place. He made a total of 24 appearances for United without scoring a single goal. He later played for Blackburn Rovers, where he did become a crowd favourite.

RUTHERFORD, JACK. Playing his first match as a 17-year-old, Rutherford was the youngest United debutant of the time. He was an outstanding talent and one of the most influential signings the club has ever made. A right-winger, he arrived from Willington Athletic in 1902 and clocked up 334 appearances and 92 goals for United. Rutherford was a demon on the ball; he was difficult to knock off it, and hard to pursue. He forged an electric partnership with Jimmy Howie – the pair complemented each other perfectly, with Howie sending Jackie on his winding runs and looking for the return ball in the opponents' penalty-area. Their partnership was so renowned that the opposition would often plan their defensive tactics around this pair alone. Jackie Rutherford's association with the Magpies ended in rather a bitter manner with a number of disputes over benefits, rewards and such like. Many clubs were rewarding their loyal stars with such payments, such as the testimonials of today. When Newcastle refused to recognise Jackie's contribution in this way, a great partnership came to an end.

S

SANSOM, KENNY. England international full-back who joined United from Arsenal in 1988. He remained on Tyneside for just one season. Sansom struggled to meet the standards set at St James's Park and was released to join Queens Park Rangers in 1989. He made 24 appearances and scored no goals.

SAUNDERS, WESLEY. Central-defender who emerged through the United juniors, Saunders was a useful player with a good football brain. Sadly he lacked goal power and was apt to make the odd costly error. He moved to Carlisle United after a loan spell with Bradford City in 1985 and went on to play for Dundee and Torquay. He made 93 appearances scoring only one goal.

SCANLON, ALBERT. The nephew of ex-United manager Charlie Mitten, Scanlon arrived from Manchester United for an £18,000 fee in late 1960. The dashing Scanlon had seen the awful tragedy of Munich with the Busby Babes, which seriously affected his football career. An outside-left, he had made five England U-23 appearances. He played in 27 first-team matches for United and scored six goals. He was never the player he had been with the

Manchester club, however, and was sold to Lincoln City in February 1962.

SCORER. Jackie Milburn is one of an élite band to have scored a goal in every round of the FA Cup in one season's competition. Milburn's goals came in the success of 1951 and were against Bury, Bolton (2), Stoke, Bristol Rovers, Wolverhampton Wanderers, and Blackpool (2).

SCOTT, JAMES. Winger and brother of Everton star Alex Scott, Jimmy Scott was purchased from Hibernian in August 1967 having impressed United with his pace and finesse on the ball. Scott had an exquisite way of leaving defenders in his wake; his almost arrogant touch could at times equal the best in the world. He was a master at running on to a ball and crossing on the run. He made one Scottish international appearance and played 92 games (six more as a substitute) and scored 12 goals for United. He was sold to Crystal Palace in February 1970.

SCOTT, JAMES. A forward who rose through the apprentice ranks, Scott made nine first-team starts with one more as substitute between 1976 and 1980. This was a difficult time to be a striker on United's books as competition for the position was strong.

SCOTT, KEVIN. Easington-born defender now playing for Tottenham Hotspur, Scott was another junior who made it all the way. He scored on his first-team debut, against Sheffield Wednesday, in 1986. Tall and well-built, he lacked a good first touch and, like many players of his type, made the odd blunder. Scott was a bit of a clumsy footballer, but his heart was as big as an ox. Few players would put as much as he did into a game. One colleague described him as a 'big friendly giant'. Unfortunately his style of play is all too common in today's game so he will never be a truly outstanding footballer, but rather one who would be a welcome part of any club side. Between 1984 and 1994 he made 260 appearances for Newcastle, with one further as a substitute, and scored nine goals.

Kevin Scott

SCOTT, MALCOLM. A first-class cricketer with Northants, Scott's real football career began when he signed professional terms for United from local football in September 1955. After only 25 appearances and two goals for United, the centre-half was sold to Darlington in October 1961.

SCOTTISH INFLUENCE. On 6 October 1928, United faced Leeds United in a League fixture. Of the eleven players in the Newcastle line-up ten were Scottish! Wood, the centre-half, was the odd one out – he was Welsh! Incidentally, United beat Leeds 3–2.

SCOULAR, JAMES. Hard-working and determined team leader, Scoular signed for United from Portsmouth in June 1953 for a fee of around £26,000. Scoular quickly took over the team captaincy and led United to FA Cup success in 1955. A tireless worker in the Magpies' midfield, he was surrounded by players of supreme quality and never regretted his move to the North East. After 271 games and six goals, he moved to Bradford Park Avenue in January 1961, where he took over as player-manager. Scoular had a good career in club management with Cardiff City for nine years, and later with Newport County. He also acted as a scout for Newcastle in 1978.

SELLARS, SCOTT. Signed from Leeds United, this slightly-built midfielder possesses so much skill and ability that it almost seems to confuse him at times. Sellars has the uncanny knack of playing world-class passes with just the slightest touch of his foot. At Leeds he trained under Eddie Gray – himself a first-class player with a celebrated left foot. Sellars then moved to Blackburn only to return to Leeds when Howard Wilkinson took up the reins, but he was never given the opportunity to prove himself in the new Leeds side. Kevin Keegan snapped him up in 1993, and although his career has been badly disrupted through injury, there are few better left-sided midfield players in today's Premier League.

SEMI-FINAL SCORES. Newcastle are one of just three clubs to score six goals in an FA Cup semi-final. Their 6–0 victory was against Fulham at Anfield in 1908.

SENDING-OFF. One the Newcastle manager will want to forget. Kevin Keegan is one of just six footballers to be sent off at Wembley. As a Liverpool player, he was shown the red card after an altercation with Leeds captain Billy Bremner in the 1975 FA Charity Shield. Both players removed their shirts as they walked off the pitch as a sign of the shame they felt they had brought upon their clubs.

SEYMOUR, STANLEY. Seymour has lived out every schoolboy's dream, having played for, managed and been a Director and Chairman of Newcastle United in an association with the club which lasted well over 50 years. Incredibly, after trials with the club as an amateur, he was judged to be too small and was released, signing for

Scott Sellars

Bradford City in September 1911. A short time later, in February 1913, he moved to Scotland's Greenock Morton. As a left-winger he was outstanding in his seven years service for the Scottish club. He was signed by Newcastle in May 1920 – and the rest, as they say, is history. Seymour won a League Championship medal with United in 1927 and an FA Cup-winners' medal in 1924. He retired from playing in May 1929 and concentrated on running a sports shop in the city. In June 1938 he joined the United board of directors, where he remained until 1976. As manager, he had two spells at the club, the first between September 1939 and March 1947, the second from December 1950 until December 1954, when he took over as club Chairman. As United's manager, he led his side to two successful FA Cup finals, in 1951 and 1952. Stan Seymour remained as a Director and Vice-President of United until April 1976, and his son, Stan, was also Chairman of the club for a time. No one has done as much for Newcastle United FC as this man, who dedicated his whole life to the betterment of the Magpies.

Stan Seymour passed away on 24 December 1978. Gone but not forgotten, his total appearances for the club stands at 266 matches, with 84 goals scored.

SHACKLETON, LEN. Bradford-born forward, 'Shack' had outstanding ability as a footballer. After appearing for Arsenal in the Wartime League, he signed for his local side, Bradford Park Avenue, where he made seven League appearances and scored four goals. In October 1946 he arrived at St James's Park and scored six times on his debut, against Newport County. As far as the fans were concerned, it was a case of instant adulation. The sight of Shack tearing towards defences with the ball at his feet is an image that will linger for years in the memory of many United supporters, Then, tragedy struck: February 1948 saw the announcement no supporter of United will ever forget. Shack was to be sold to Sunderland, having played 64 games and scored 29 goals. It has to be said that his career really did take off at Roker Park where he made more than 300 appearances and scored over 100 goals. International recognition came with five full England caps, and one England 'B' cap. Few players inspired as much as Shackleton and it was a great shame he couldn't remain with United for a longer spell.

SHEEDY, KEVIN. Sheedy made his name with Hereford, Liverpool and Everton. A midfielder, he had won international recognition with the Republic of Ireland, and was well known for his ability to score brilliant goals from long distances. He made a total of 42 appearances for Newcastle between 1992 and 1993, as well as two substitute appearances, and scored five goals.

SHEPHERD, ALBERT. Signed by United on the basis of his reputation as the top striker in the country at the time. Shepherd arrived at St James's Park in 1908 from Bolton Wanderers for a fee of £800. A stocky, reasonably small forward, just 5'8", he ran and ran until he could run no more. He was incredibly quick and read the game well, which was one of the main contributory factors to his incredible scoring record – 92 goals in 123 appearances for United between 1908 and 1914. He scored on his debut against Nottingham Forest on 28 November 1908 and created numerous chances for his colleagues. It was as though he had been part of the United line-up for ever as he slotted easily into the side, just as players of such quality tend to do.

SHINTON, ROBERT. Much-travelled forward who signed from Millwall in March 1980, Shinton made 47 appearances, two as a substitute, and scored ten goals. He returned to Milwall in March 1982. His previous clubs included Walsall, Cambridge United, Wrexham and Manchester City.

SHOULDER, ALAN. With his diminutive stature and slight physique, Alan Shoulder hardly looked like a footballer. Appearances, however, can be deceptive, as Shoulder was a tremendous character both on and off the field.

He first came to light in Blyth Spartans' legendary FA Cup run of the mid-1970s. He signed for Newcastle in December 1978 and went on to score 38 goals in 106 appearances, with a further 11 as a substitute, between then and 1982. He was sold to Carlisle United, for whom he continued to excel.

SIBLEY, ALBERT. Right-winger signed from Southend United in February 1947, Sibley made 32 appearances for United and netted six goals before moving back to Southend in July 1950.

SIMPSON, RONNIE. Scottish international Ronnie Simpson was a fearless goalkeeper with a marvellous character. His consistency placed him well above the average goalkeeper. He was signed from Third Lanark in February 1951 and made 295 appearances for United between then and 1960. Hardly the biggest of men he trained and worked hard at improving his craft and was, without doubt, one of the best keepers of his day.

SINCLAIR, JACKIE. Born in Dunfermline, Jackie Sinclair had been electrifying crowds with his dribbling skills at Leicester City. After over 100 League appearances and 50 goals for the Foxes he came to Newcastle in January 1968 and made 48 first-team starts, four more as a substitute, and scored eight goals. Sinclair was an inconsistent performer who could turn a game with a flash of his natural brilliance. Although he never truly matched the form he had shown at Filbert Street, he nevertheless was a noteworthy addition to the United squad. This was especially so in the Fairs Cup triumph of 1969 when he showed what he was capable of on the European stage, scoring a vital goal against Glasgow Rangers in the semi-final victory at St James's Park. He transferred to Sheffield Wednesday in December 1969 and later signed for Chesterfield in 1973.

SMAILES, ANDREW. Blyth Spartans forward who signed for United in 1919 and went on to make 77 appearances between 1919 and 1922. Smailes was a thick-set forward who plundered defences and managed to net 30 goals in his Newcastle career. He was sold to Sheffield Wednesday for £1,500 in October 1922.

SMELLIE, RICHARD. Ex-Nottingham Forest striker who scored 15 goals for United in 27 appearances between 1896 and 1897.

SMITH, JACK. Ex-Huddersfield Town striker who was signed as a raw 19-year-old. As a former representative of England schools, he was almost immediately drafted into the first team. He went on to make 112 appearances and score 73 goals between 1934 and 1938.

SMITH, JIM. Manager from December 1988 to March 1991, nicknamed 'the Bald Eagle' by the fans. Jim Smith is a charismatic football manager known for speaking his mind. It came as something of a surprise when he agreed to join United as they were having more than their fair share of behind-the-scenes trouble. Internal politics, however, were not Jim's concern – his role was to improve the standard of football in the team. At the end of his first season United were relegated through no fault of Smith's, but it was still a major blow. The following season, they narrowly missed out on promotion and the continual behind-the-scenes bickering of that era eventually caused Smith to resign in favour of a coaching role at Middlesbrough. He returned to club management with Portsmouth in 1991. Despite his lack of success, the United faithful held Smith in high regard. They knew full well that he was a capable manager but that circumstances were against him at Newcastle.

SMITH, JIMMY. Jinky Jimmy Smith was a Glaswegian forward who arrived at St James's Park from Aberdeen in August 1969 and was to become an invaluable asset to the team. The club's first £100,000 footballer more than proved himself, playing four Scottish international matches, one U-23 match and, when he settled at the club, making 152 United appearances, seven as a substitute and scoring 13 goals between 1969 and 1976.

SMITH, NORMAN. Caretaker-manager between October 1961 and June 1962, Smith was an honest, hard-working man whose playing career was anything but spectacular, notching up barely 100 games for his three clubs. He was, however, a Newcastle man and returned to Tyneside after a brief coaching spell in Switzerland. He was employed as trainer to the first team in July 1938, a position he held until December 1962. In between this period he was made caretaker-manager after Charlie Mitten had left with the club perilously close to relegation. Smith avoided the drop but made way for Joe Harvey in June 1962 and reverted to his role as trainer.

SPEEDIE, FINLAY. In 1906 Glasgow Rangers sold Speedie to the Magpies for a huge £600 fee. Players of his ability are rare as he went on to make 59 appearances in seven different outfield positions and score 14 goals between 1906 and 1908.

SPENCER, CHARLES. Central-defender between 1921 and 1928, Spencer became an England international, gaining two caps against Scotland and Wales. He made 175 appearances for United and scored just one goal. He was a well-respected defender in his day.

SRNICEK, PAVEL. Huge 6'2" goalkeeper signed from Banik Ostrava in January 1991. Pavel is now the confirmed first-choice keeper and has an excellent reputation. The longer he stays in England the more his confidence grows and the more his performance improves. Occasionally there is the odd hiccup, like the soft goal he let in against Liverpool in a 1–1 draw at St James's Park in 1994. However, these are more than balanced by exceptional performances such as those against Leeds or Blackburn. Srnicek is undoubtedly one of the top keepers in the Premiership.

STARLING, RONALD. Young striker who signed for United in 1930, Starling had few inspirational performances but was a good provider who fought hard to keep his place. He made 53 first-team outings and scored eight goals between 1930 and 1932.

Pavel Srnicek

STEPHENSON, PAUL. United apprentice who made his first-team debut in December 1985 at home to Southampton. A forward, his solitary United goal came in that same season in a 4–1 win over Sheffield Wednesday. He made 63 appearances, four as a substitute, and scored one goal between 1984 and 1988 before a move to Millwall.

STEWART, IAN. A defender who signed from Queens Park Rangers in 1985, Stewart was a solid and reliable Northern Ireland international. He was able to make difficult things look easy and was something of the joker in the pack. He was renowned around St James's Park for his caricatures and cartoon-style sketches of his colleagues. He moved to Portsmouth in 1987 after having made 40 appearances, ten more as a substitute, and scored three goals.

STEWART, JAMES. 'Tadger' Stewart arrived from Sheffield Wednesday in 1908 and was a capable goalscorer. Another England international he made 138 appearances and scored 53 goals for United. An early photograph of him in his England attire makes him look like Eric Cantona!

STIMSON, MARK. Defender who graduated through Tottenham Hotspur's ranks before transferring to United in 1989. A solid defender, he went on to make 94 first-team appearances, with four more as a substitute, and scored three goals, the first being in a 3–2 home defeat by Oxford United in 1989. He was sold to Portsmouth in 1992 where he rejoined his ex-United manager Jim Smith. Stimson was a good defender but at that stage perhaps not quite good enough for the challenge of Premiership football.

STOBBART, GEORGE. Signed from Middlesbrough in September 1946, Stobbart was a striker: 22 goals in 72 appearances between 1946 and his move to Luton Town in December 1949 more than proved his ability. Later he moved to Millwall and then Brentford.

STOKOE, BOB. Born in Mickley, Bob Stokoe progressed through the United juniors to sign professional terms at St James's Park in September 1947. A centre-half, he was a tower of strength, and few can understand why international recognition never came his way. Stokoe was part of the successful FA Cup campaign of 1955 and played an outstanding game in the Wembley final marking the impressive Revie out of the match. Later he moved into club management with Charlton, Bury, Blackpool, Rochdale, Carlisle and then Sunderland, and when his Sunderland team beat Leeds in 1973 he became one of the few men to have managed and played with a Cup final side. Stokoe was a leader on and off the pitch and was one of the most respected men in the game. He made 287 appearances and scored five goals for United.

STOTT, JAMES. A tough, resilient half-back who signed from Grimsby Town in 1895, Stott earned a rough-and-ready reputation for taking players out of the game with over-the-top tackles. It was a reputation which the player seems to have enjoyed, rather more than his club: Newcastle United warned him about his conduct on the field of play. He made 127 appearances and scored 11 goals between 1895 and 1899.

STUBBINS, ALBERT. Between 1937 and 1946 Stubbins was the country's most lethal goalscorer. A huge man who packed a powerful shot he could intimidate opposing defences and goalkeepers with his aerial challenges and deadly accurate shooting. Much of his Newcastle career took place during the war so officially he made just 30 appearances and scored six goals. However, his Wartime League record is unbelievable: 188 games and 231 goals! Granted some of the opposition was weaker then than the usual Football League standards, but Stubbins' record is still outstanding.

SUCCESS. The Magpies are the seventh most successful English League club of all time, with 13 domestic and European trophies to their credit. Chronologically these are:
League Champions: 1905, 1907, 1909, 1927
Division 2 Champions: 1965
FA Cup-winners: 1910, 1924, 1932, 1951, 1952, 1955
Charity Shield-winners: 1909
Inter Cities Fairs Cup-winners: 1969.

SUDDICK, ALAN. A creative midfielder, Alan Suddick was a consistent performer who played very few poor matches. He was a tough tackler who enjoyed his game and instilled confidence in all those around him. He signed professional terms in October 1961 and went on to make 152 appearances and score 43 goals. He then transferred to Blackpool in December 1966, where he became the mainstay of the team for over 300 games.

SUGGETT, COLIN. Born in the North East, Suggett spent most of his playing career in the Midlands and East Anglia.

Initially signed by Sunderland in 1966, he was sold to West Bromwich Albion in July 1969. After many inspired performances in the Baggies midfield he was signed by Norwich in February 1973. Over 200 games and 20-plus goals later he arrived at Newcastle in August 1978. Perhaps past his youthful prime, Suggett still possessed a wealth of experience which was barely used in his 21 appearances for the club, three more as a substitute. Suggett had a great influence upon the United side both on and off the field, and although his playing days for the club were limited between 1978 and 1981, he worked behind-the-scenes maintaining his influence.

SWEENEY, PAUL. A midfield capture from Raith Rovers in 1989, Sweeney was another hard-working player who was more enthusiastic than skilful. In Scotland he had looked good, very good in fact, but at Newcastle he seemed average, almost as though he was overawed by St James's Park. He made 33 appearances with a further nine matches on the substitute bench. He was transferred to St Johnstone in 1990, his undoubted talent lost to the English game.

SWINBURNE, THOMAS. Swinburne's career as Newcastle's goalkeeper was disrupted by the outbreak of war. A well-built man, he did manage to make 84 first-class appearances for the club between 1934 and 1947. Added to this were 51 Wartime League appearances. He was the first in a long line of top-quality keepers to play for United.

T

TAIT, ALEX. An England youth international centre-forward, Tait was born and bred in Bedlington and came through the United juniors, signing professional terms in September 1952. He scored ten goals in his 34 games for Newcastle. He was sold to Bristol City in June 1960 and turned out later for Doncaster Rovers.

TAPKEN, NORMAN. A local lad signed from Wallsend Thermal Welfare in 1933, Tapken was a goalkeeper, and a good one at that. He made 113 outings for the United first team between 1933 and 1938. After the war he returned but was eventually signed by Manchester United before moving to Darlington in April 1947.

TAYLOR, COLIN. A Midlands-born left-winger, Taylor's career began with Walsall where he made well over 200 appearances and netted over 90 goals. He was transferred to United in June 1963. He was something of a disappointment – he remained at the club until October 1964 making 36 appearances and scoring only seven goals. He was homesick and so was sold back to Wallsall.

TAYLOR, ERNEST. Forward signed during the wartime years, Taylor was a real flyer. He possessed instant pace and was a consistently good performer. He played in 117 games and scored 21 goals before being sold to Blackpool in October 1951. Taylor went on to attain England international honours.

TAYLOR, HENRY. Another local-born forward, Henry Taylor signed from the United junior ranks in November 1952. He made 29 starts and scored five goals between 1952 and 1960. He also had a brief loan spell with Fulham where he played four games in 1957 without scoring.

TEMPLETON, ROBERT. Signed in a £400 transfer from Aston Villa in 1903, Templeton was a high-profile player. A Scottish international, he had the confidence to try the impossible. Off the field he once placed his head in a lion's mouth at a circus and allegedly received a medal for his bravery! On the field he made 52 appearances and scored five goals in 1903–4.

THOMAS, ANDREW. Ex-Oxford United forward who had spent loan spells at Fulham and Derby County. He arrived at Newcastle in 1986 and made his first-team debut playing alongside Paul Gascoigne against Wimbledon in September 1986. In 28 first-team outings, seven more as a substitute, he scored seven goals before moving on to Bradford City in 1988.

THOMAS, BARRIE. Much-travelled centre-forward who had gained England youth international honours whilst with Leicester City. He moved on to Mansfield Town then Scunthorpe United before signing for the Magpies in January 1962 for a £40,000 fee. A well-proven goalscorer, he suffered injury problems whilst at St James's Park which limited his appearances to 78. However, a healthy 50 goals were scored before he returned to Scunthorpe United in November 1964.

THOMAS, MARTIN. Welsh goalkeeper who had earned a marvellous reputation keeping clean sheets at Bristol

Rovers. He spent loan spells with Cardiff City and Southend United as well as United before finally signing in March 1983. Although a good shot-stopper and reflex keeper he is prone to lapses of concentration when given time to contemplate a save. Thomas made 130 outings for United before being sold to Birmingham City in 1988.

THOMPSON, JOHN. Newcastle-born keeper John Thompson was an acrobatic goalie who spent much of his time in the reserves. Signed through the juniors in September 1950, he made just eight appearances in the first team before being transferred to Lincoln City in May 1957.

THOMPSON, ROBERT. Full-back signed from Sunderland as part of a player-exchange deal between the two clubs with Robert McKay going in the opposite direction. Thompson had earned one Scottish international cap in 1927 whilst a player for Falkirk and went on to make 80 appearances for United in six years' service between 1928 and 1934.

THOMPSON, THOMAS. 'Toucher' Thompson was signed via Lumley YMCA in August 1946. A neat and sensible inside-forward, he made 20 appearances for the club, scoring six goals. He was transferred to Aston Villa in August 1950 and went on to make a number of England full international appearances. He later played for Preston, Stoke City and Barrow.

THOMPSON, WILLIAM. A centre-half and yet another product of the excellent junior team who signed professional terms in January 1957 and remained in the club for ten years, making 88 appearances, one as a substitute, and scored once. A typically lean, no-nonsense centre-half and ball-winner.

THOMPSON, WILLIAM. Willie Thompson, moustache and all, was the club's first-ever centre-forward – the first man to wear that now legendary number-9 jersey. Ex-Black Watch (Shankhouse), he was a demon in front of goal,

THE ST JAMES'S PARK ENCYCLOPEDIA

especially for a man who was not the tallest in the game. He took part in United's first-ever League game, against Arsenal. Between 1892 and 1897 he made 91 appearances and scored 40 goals.

THORN, ANDREW. Signed from Wimbledon, Thorn was without doubt a class act. Superb in the tackle and in his distribution, he possessed a gritty determination which made him a winner. A defender, he made 40 appearances and scored three goals for Newcastle, before being sold to Crystal Palace in 1989.

TICKETS. United featured in the first-ever all-ticket FA Cup final against Aston Villa on 26 April 1924 when 100,000 fans saw the Magpies lift the trophy after beating Villa 2–0.

TINNION, BRIAN. This apprentice, who signed professional and went on to make his debut in the 1986–87 season, was first used as a winger but later dropped back to left-back where he proved himself to be more than capable. Tinnion made 35 appearances, plus two as a substitute, and scored two goals. A useful player, his skills were noticed by Bradford City who took him to Valley Parade in the 1988–89 season. He later moved to Bristol City in 1992.

TOON ARMY. The fanatical following which United take to each and every game, home or away, is now affectionately called the Toon Army. The vociferous support the Toons provide for the club is, some pundits tell us, worth a goal-start in any game.

TOUR SUCCESS. No United tour has been as successful as that which took place after the 1952 FA Cup final success when the club embarked upon a gruelling South African series of dates. Overall there were 16 games played, 15 of which were won. To prove their worldwide ability, the team also bagged some 73 goals!

The Toon Army

TRANSFER RECORDS. The club set a new transfer record in October 1928 when they paid £8,000 for Burnley's flame-haired centre-half Jack Hill. This is peanuts when one considers that the club broke their own transfer record in March 1994 when they paid out a collosal £2,700,000 for a Queens Park Rangers centre-half, Darren Peacock. Even this fades into insignificance when compared to the whopping £7,000,000-plus-player exchange from Manchester United for superstriker Andy Cole. This is a record which I am certain will stand for some time.

TREWICK, JOHN. Originally from Bedlington, Trewick was signed as an apprentice by West Bromwich Albion in July 1974. He was an England youth international as well as a schools representative who made over 90 appearances for his first club, scoring over 11 goals. He was signed by

Newcastle in December 1980 to bolster the midfield and to wade in with the odd goal from his midfield position. Trewick did everything that was asked of him and was a good club servant, making 85 appearances (two more as a substitute) and bagging eight goals. He was sold to the rapidly improving Oxford United in 1984 after an earlier loan spell.

TUDOR, JOHN. Goal, goal, goal! John Tudor had but one idea when he signed for Newcastle from Sheffield United in January 1971. He had been bought to score goals and that was all he wanted to do. There was no messing about with Tudor, no lack of confidence, and this explains why the fans loved him so much. Brilliant in the air, lethal on the floor, he had everything – yet for so long played second-fiddle to another great striker, SuperMac. The pair were deadly. Tudor supplied and weighed in with his fair share but it was generally SuperMac who got the glory. Tudor seemed to feed off this and improved as he matured. After 184 appearances (three as a substitute) and 58 goals, he was disappointingly sold to Stoke City in September 1976. How the United fans loved to sing his name over and over again: 'Tudor, Tudor, Tudor!', they would cry. And the 'mighty John' would respond all the more. He first signed as a professional player with Coventry City in January 1966 and his goals graced the game for just ten years. He was a wonderful striker.

TUOHY, LIAM. As a winger signed from Shamrock Rovers in May 1960, Liam was so quick that his pace often caught out defenders – but it also caught out Liam himself sometimes as his sudden bursts with the ball would see him running on beyond the goal-line. After 42 appearances and nine goals between 1960 and 1963, he returned to Shamrock Rovers. He gained two full caps for the Republic of Ireland whilst at Newcastle.

TURNER, ARTHUR. A forward who signed from Southampton, Turner was in the twilight of his playing career by the time he reached Newcastle. He was a stop-gap striker at the club and made just 13 appearances with one goal in season 1903–4. He was an England international with two full caps whilst with the Saints.

TURNER, DAVID. Wing-half whose career began at St James's Park when he signed professional in October 1960. He made just 3 appearances without scoring a goal before being sold to Brighton and Hove Albion in December 1963 where he went on to make over 300 appearances for the Seagulls. Later he was sold to Blackburn Rovers.

U

UNBELIEVABLE. Kevin Keegan never once scored in a Merseyside derby fixture, which is amazing when one considers that he scored 100 goals in his time at Liverpool!

When Duncan Hutchison signed from Dundee United in 1929, some 300 Dundee fans travelled down from Tayside to witness his debut. They presented the player with a good luck medal! How refreshing, when today many former players are rebuked by their previous club's supporters.

When United won the Fairs Cup in 1969, they qualified through having finished in tenth position in Division 1 the year before. It was usually the top four who entered European competition but fate was on United's side that season.

UNITED. Newcastle are one of just 15 'Uniteds' operating in the League. They are arguably the second-oldest United in existence in the professional leagues, beaten only by Manchester United.

URWIN, THOMAS. An international winger signed from Middlesbrough in 1924, Urwin could operate from either wing and was accurate with crosses from either boot. The move from Boro had come after a disagreement over payments, which suited Newcastle fine as he made 200 appearances, scoring 24 goals, between 1924 and 1930. He later moved to Sunderland.

V

VARADI, IMRE. Having started his career at Sheffield United, Varadi moved to Everton before arriving on Tyneside in August 1981. A striker with a keen eye for goal Varadi was devastatingly lethal: 90 appearances and 42 goals stand as proof of his scoring prowess. He was a hard-working forward just as capable of creating chances for colleagues as of finishing them off himself. Since transferring to Sheffield Wednesday in August 1983 he has been a frequent traveller, scoring goals for West Bromwich Albion, Manchester City, Leeds United, Luton, Oxford and Rotherham.

VEITCH, COLIN. Colin Campbell McKechnie Veitch was born in Newcastle in 1881 and signed as an amateur for his local club side in 1899 before finally turning professional in 1903. His professional playing days were all spent at St James's Park where he made 321 appearances and scored 49 goals before retiring in 1915.

In 1918 he took over as United's first-team coach before running the Swifts, the club's nursery team, between 1924 and 1926. Management seemed a natural progression and he took over at Bradford City as manager/secretary in August 1926 until January 1928.

Veitch the player was far more successful than Veitch the manager; an England international with six caps, a Football League Representative with four caps, and a Football League Champion in 1905, 1907 and 1909, he also won FA Cup-winners' honours in 1910 and was a runner-up in 1905, 1906, 1908 and 1911.

Words cannot describe just how good Colin Veitch actually was: composed, intellectual and enthusiastic about everything he did, he was a United man with the interests of Newcastle closest to his heart. A real Geordie, Veitch passed away in Switzerland in 1938. Long may his memory survive.

VENISON, BARRY. A former Liverpool and Sunderland defender, Barry Venison was much-loved by the Newcastle fans. His successful career at St James's came to a halt in the summer of 1995 when Graeme Souness persuaded him to sign for Galatasaray, the Turkish side he now manages. It's easy to see why Souness went after him: 'Veno' was probably the most influential footballer United had at the time. As cool a player as you will find, he is not easily flustered and this seems to provide his colleagues with the confidence to go out and win. He was more than capable of scoring goals himself: remember the one he cracked home against Aston Villa in February 1995? Alternately, the off-the-line clearance he made in the 1994 FA Cup-tie at Luton Town was as good as you will ever see – a spectacular flying overhead kick. His appearance speaks volumes for his character – long flowing locks, outrageous suits which, strangely, look good on him. He is a players' player, and an idol to the fans.

VICTORIES. United's biggest-ever home victory was against Newport County in a Division 2 fixture on 5 October 1946 – United were the eventual 13–0 winners! The record away victory stands at six clear goals, at Everton and Walsall on 26 October 1912 and 29 September 1962 respectively. More pertinently, there is also a 7–1 victory over Manchester United on 10 September 1927.

VITORIA SETUBAL. The club who faced United in the fourth round of the 1968–69 Fairs Cup competition. The home tie was a formality, with United winning 5–1, with goals by Davies, Foggon, Gibb and B. Robson (2). Vitoria actually won the second leg 3–1, with United's sole reply coming from Wyn Davies. United sailed through 6–4 on aggregate.

Barry Venison

W

WADDLE, CHRIS. Signed from Tow Law Town in July 1980, Chrissy was plucked from obscurity as a sausage-maker to become a world-class soccer player. A tall player, he likes to play out on the left and loves nothing more than having the ball at his feet with defenders in front of him. More often than not he would weave in and out and chip or curl a precise ball into the opposing penalty-area. At Brunton Park, Carlisle, when Waddle once bent a precise ball into the top left-hand corner of the Cumbrians' net, the movement of his foot was hardly noticeable. It earned Waddle a standing ovation from some of his greatest critics. Waddle looks remarkably gangly but appearances can be deceptive. He is in fact well balanced and is more comfortable on the ball than many players in today's game. When United boasted a side with Waddle, Keegan, McDermott and co., it is easy to see why the crowds flocked to see them. In 1985 Chrissy said goodbye to Newcastle after 190 games, one more as a substitute, and 52 goals. He joined Tottenham Hotspur, where he matured, before making a move abroad with Marseille. He was adored in France but the lure of home shores was too much for him to resist. In 1992 he transferred to Sheffield Wednesday where his class still shines through at the age of 34. There has been

189

talk of a player-manager's role elsewhere in the League but whatever Chris decides to do, he has had an outstanding playing career and was one of the best of his time.

WALKER, NIGEL. Midfielder signed from local non-League side Whickham in July 1977, Walker was a shrewd footballer who read and played the game to the best of his undoubted ability. Between 1977 and 1982 he made 69 first-team outings, five as a substitute, and scored three goals. After a brief spell with San Diego, he joined Sunderland in December 1982, drifting in and out of the game with several other clubs.

WALKER, THOMAS. An outside-right, Walker signed from Netherton shortly after the war. He progressively improved as time went by and managed to make 204 appearances for the club, scoring 38 goals. A rare talent, he served United well before being sold to Oldham Athletic in February 1954. His best days, however, had been at St James's Park.

WALLACE, JAMES. Winger and goalscorer who played in United's first-ever League fixture. Of slim build, Wallace was clearly a handful for any defence – in his 45 appearances he managed to score 21 goals between 1890 and 1895.

WALLACE, JOSEPH. A slimline Scot, Wallace was United's first-ever left-winger, who appeared in the opening League fixture. With 45 appearances and 21 goals to his credit, he was sharp around the opposition goal, ferreting out and creating goals for his colleagues.

WARD, EDWARD. Blyth striker who signed for United in 1920 and went on to make 25 appearances and score five goals for the club before being released in 1922.

WARD, WILLIAM. Goalkeeper signed from Loughborough Town in 1894 who was neither dominant nor spectacular, but whose enthusiasm and self-motivation carried him through. At Loughborough he forged a great defensive role for himself. He made 21 appearances for Newcastle between 1894 and 1896.

WARDROPE, WILLIAM. A non-League striker, signed from Wishaw in 1895, Wardrope was renowned for his furious pace and dashing, cutting runs inside defenders. He represented the Scottish Football League, was a frequent goalscorer and a real crowd favourite who made 141 appearances between 1895 and 1900, scoring 50 goals.

WARE, HAROLD. Slick utility player signed by Tom Mather for a fee of £2,400 from Stoke City. Ware was a player of outstanding quality – not a star but a team member – whose contribution on a weekly basis tended to go unnoticed by the average fan. Ware was Mr Consistency during his two-year spell at the club between 1935 and 1937 making 49 appearances and scoring 9 goals.

WATSON, STEVE. A star for the future, Watson has staked his claim for a permanent place in the United first team. A strong midfielder with a liking for forward forays deep into opposition territory, his ball-control and skill make him a tricky customer. In defence, he is solid and quick to make decisions. A long-throw specialist, he was signed in July 1990 from Wallsend Boys Club.

WATTS, CHARLES. Signed in 1896 from Burton Wanderers, Watts was an extrovert character who, though a crowd-pleaser, was a manager's nightmare. Watts enjoyed an audience and would play to one, as in goal he was as good as there was, making a total of 97 first-team appearances for United between 1896 and 1906. Watts was also known as something of a gambling man. His racing tips earned him some notoriety, as did his suicide in 1924 when he cut his own throat. It was a sad end for a marvellous character, but Watts always seemed determined to make the headlines.

WATT, FRANK. Secretary/manager 1896–1930. The most successful of all the club's leaders, Frank Watt worked miracles at Newcastle United. A former referee, he took over team affairs in 1896 and transformed the club into a trophy-winner. During his reign he won the League Championship (1905, 1907, 1909 and 1927), promotion from the second division (1898), the FA Cup (1910 and 1924), FA Cup runners-up medals (1905, 1906, 1908, and 1911), and the FA Charity Shield (1909). This is a fantastic record by a fantastic man. Frank Watt laid the foundations for the Newcastle United we know today.

Steve Watson

WAYMAN, CHARLES. Born in Bishop Auckland, Wayman was small for a striker but was a precise and clinical finisher. Signed after the Second World War, he made 53 first-class, appearances scoring 36 goals. However, a bust-up with the United management, who saw fit to drop him from the FA Cup semi-final side, was the final straw for both sides; United lost the game 4–0, and Wayman asked for a move. He was sold to Southampton in October 1947 and later played for Preston, Middlesbrough and Darlington.

WEAVER, SAMUEL. An England international with three full caps and a representative of the English Football League, Sammy Weaver was a fine wing-half. He was initially signed for Sutton Town before moving to Hull City and Newcastle United in 1929 for a fee of £2,500. He scored the winning goal in a 1–0 victory over Arsenal at Highbury on his debut on 30 November 1929. His astute distribution of the ball and tenacious tackling were consistently good. He won an FA Cup-winners' medal in 1932 before dropping out through injury. He signed for Chelsea in 1936 having made 229 appearances and scored 43 goals for the Magpies. He retired from playing in 1947 whilst on Stockport County's books. During the war, which decimated his football career, he guested for Derby, Mansfield, West Ham, Notts County, Leeds, Fulham, Wrexham and Stockport. When his playing days ended he joined the coaching staff at Leeds United and then Millwall in 1949. He finally moved to Mansfield Town after a brief association with Bromley.

WHARTON, KENNY. A midfielder who signed from Grainger Park Boys Club in January 1979, Wharton was a hard, no-nonsense player who gave his heart for 90 minutes every time he donned the United shirt. Newcastle-born and bred, he progressed to make 303 appearances, with 24 more as a substitute, and scored 27 goals. Kenny was a well-liked player who always made time to speak to United fans. Equally well respected on the pitch, he was very much an ambassador for the club, enjoying his game but maintaining a discreet role in the side. He was transferred to

Middlesbrough in the 1989–90 season before a brief liaison with Carlisle, Bradford City and West Bromwich Albion.

WHITE, JOHN. Ex-Clyde defender John White signed for Newcastle in 1896 and slotted straight into the side, where he formed a neat partnership with his colleague Tom Stewart. Both were Scots and could read each other's game and pattern of play instinctively. White made 53 appearances and scored one goal between 1896 and 1898.

WHITE, LEN. A sturdy and complete forward, Len White was signed from Rotherham United in February 1953. He took his time to break through into a regular first-team position and was more of a utility man at first. However, by 1954–55, he had made a name for himself as a crafty goalscorer. The centre-forward position was held by Jackie Milburn so White was used as a feeder or supplier to the great man. He appeared in the 1955 FA Cup final and it was from his corner-kick that Milburn buried United's opening goal. After Jackie's retirement, Len White took over his mantle as centre-forward and carried the responsibility very well, cracking in goal after goal. Between 1953 and 1962 he made a total of 269 first-team outings and scored 153 goals. In January 1962 he was sold to Huddersfield Town and three years later moved to Stockport County. White was a player who captivated audiences with his goal-scoring exploits wherever he played.

WHITEHEAD, ROBERT. Arriving via Fairfield Athletic in December 1954, Whitehouse didn't make his first-team debut until the 1957–58 season. A full-back, he never seemed to fit into the manager's plans and made only 20 appearances between signing on and 1962, when he was sold to Darlington for a nominal fee.

WHITEHURST, WILLIAM. Large and extremely powerful centre-forward, Billy Whitehurst made his name at Hull City before joining United in the 1985–86 season. Good in the air and with an explosive shot, Whitehurst was a typical, old-fashioned striker, powering his huge frame

Billy Whitehurst

into every tackle and challenge. His time at Newcastle was not particularly fruitful – he made just 30 appearances, one as a substitute and scored seven goals. He later played for Oxford, Reading, Sunderland, Hull City (again), Sheffield United, Stoke City, Doncaster and Crewe, before finally drifting into the non-League game where his outstanding career probably hit rock-bottom when signed by a poor and struggling Kettering Town side. Whitehurst was a character both on and off the field, committed to everything he did and a genuine man into the bargain.

WHITSON, ANTHONY. Cape Town-born full-back who moved to the North East as a child. This smart and capable defender who was full of ability was a true professional who cared about his every move on the football field, and trained hard to maintain standards. He made 145 appearances without a goal between 1905 and 1919.

WILLIAMS, RONALD. Signed from Swansea Town as yet another goalscorer, Ronnie Williams cost the club a fee of £1,500. On his debut on 25 November 1933 he scored a goal at Villa Park when Newcastle won 3–2. An international, he made two appearances for Wales whilst with the club. He managed 36 appearances and scored 14 goals in his spell on Tyneside.

WILLIS, DAVID. Strong, agile central defender Dave Willis from Byker was signed from Sunderland in a £100 deal. Very little got past this giant figure of a man. He became a vital cog in the United defence for several years and made 107 appearances scoring four goals between 1907 and 1913.

WILSON, GEORGE. A record signing from Everton, Wilson cost the princely sum of £1,600 when United stepped in to snap him up after internal politics had caused him to seek a transfer from the Toffeemen. Wilson was an individual who disliked the system. He refused to conform but was as loyal a servant as one could have hoped for when he came to St James's Park. Known as a constant moaner, his colleagues nicknamed him 'Smiler'. He had a Newcastle career total of 217 appearances and 33 goals.

WILSON, JAMES. Defender from Shotts BA who signed in September 1959. Made his debut in the 1960–61 season and played 13 games, scoring two goals, before he left the club in 1962.

WILSON, JOSEPH. Ex-Tanfield Lea, Wilson was a youngster who was tried out during a three-year spell but remained firmly in the reserves. A midfielder, he made 30 appearances and scored five goals between 1933 and 1936.

WILSON, WILLIAM. Wilson made a somewhat nervous start to his United career when he was signed from Peebles Rovers in 1925. Goalkeepers are always in a position where mistakes can cost their side dearly. Wilson, though clearly a little overawed upon his arrival, went on to prove himself more than capable as a first-rate stopper. Between 1925 and 1929 he made 134 appearances and won a Championship medal with the club in 1927.

WINSTANLEY, GRAHAM. 'Tot' Winstanley was a tall and effective centre-half who signed as an apprentice and progressed to professional terms in December 1968. He was always going to struggle to get into a side which had arguably one of the best defences in the land, but still managed to notch up seven first-team outings, with two more as a substitute. He was sold to Carlisle United in August 1969.

WITHE, PETER. Strong, athletic centre-forward, Peter Withe was born in Liverpool and signed for Southport in 1971. From there he moved to Barrow, Wolverhampton Wanderers, Birmingham City and Nottingham Forest, before Newcastle signed him in August 1978. Withe had made an excellent name for himself with Birmingham and Forest which was to continue on Tyneside. Some 83 appearances and 27 goals later, he was on the move again, this time to Aston Villa where he won domestic and

European honours. Withe looked mean but was totally the opposite; he had a splendid sense of humour and was the first to praise the fans. He was missed when he departed to Villa Park.

WOODBURN, JAMES. Born in Rutherglen, Woodburn signed for Coltness United before moving into the professional game with Newcastle in 1946. A left-half, he remained at St James's for just two seasons without doing himself justice. He made 47 appearances and scored four goals before moving to Gateshead in September 1948.

WOODS, CHARLES. Whitehaven-born inside-forward, Woods was signed from Cleator Moor Celtic in May 1959 and managed to bridge the gap from non-League to professional football quite easily. He made 30 outings for the first team and snatched ten goals into the bargain. He was eventually sold to Bournemouth in November 1962.

WOOLARD, ARNOLD. Born in Wales, Woolard was first signed by Northampton Town in 1949 as a full-back. He made only three outings for the Cobblers before signing for Newcastle in December 1952. He struggled on Tyneside and was less than impressive when given his opportunity – he managed just ten outings between 1952 and 1956. He was sold to Bournemouth in June 1956.

WRIGHT, BRIAN. Sunderland-born Brian Wright was brought to Newcastle as a junior and progressed to sign professional in September 1956. A solid, keen player, he did well at the club and never looked out of place in the first team. He made 47 appearances and scored one goal before being sold to Peterborough United in May 1963.

WRIGHT, DOUGLAS. Signed from Southend in 1938, Wright cost United a fee of £3,250 but, as a master of his trade, he was worth every penny. Totally dominant in midfield, he seemed to caress the ball with his feet as he carved open the opposition time and again with cleverly weighted passes and piercing through-balls. As well as playing for England, he made some 82 appearances for Newcastle and scored one goal.

WRIGHT, THOMAS. Irish international Tommy Wright had the makings of a first-class goalkeeper. Making his United debut in a 3–1 defeat by Aston Villa in 1988, he had some awful luck in the United goal. His frailties were often captured by television cameras which seemed to be a bad omen for him. Although competent at shot-stopping, he seemed incapable of decision-making in his own box, which kept him mainly in the United reserves until his sale to Nottingham Forest in 1993. Wright made 82 outings, plus one more as a substitute, between 1988 and 1993.

XMAS HOLIDAY BONANZA. During the Christmas holiday period of 1933–34 United faced tough opposition in the form of Everton and Liverpool. The first fixture was at Goodison Park where the club amazingly defeated the Toffeemen 7–3 with four goals coming in a five-minute spell. On New Year's Day Liverpool visited St James's Park and were trounced 9–2 with seven goals being scored in an incredible half-hour. The joy of these two outstanding Christmas presents was shortlived as United were relegated at the end of the season, having won just ten games!

X-RATED. United's X-rated opponents, according to local support, have to be Sunderland. Although both football clubs themselves have a warm, friendly and professional approach to each other the local derby is still X-rated. The two clubs are well matched in first-class fixtures: United have won 44 of these encounters and lost 41, with 40 games being drawn.

Y

YOUNG, DAVID. Newcastle-born David Young was drafted through the junior ranks as a defender, and finally signed professional in September 1964. Between 1964 and 1973 he made just 50 first-team appearances, three more as a substitute, and scored two goals. He was sold to Sunderland in January 1973 and later played for Charlton and Southend.

Z

ZENITH DATA SYSTEMS CUP. Results in this competition have been at best miserable, although one of the most exciting games of all time took place at Prenton Park, Tranmere, in an incredible 6–6 draw! Chronologically the results are:

1989–90: **Oldham Athletic** (h) won 2–0 (Quinn 2)

Derby County (h) won 3–2 (O'Brien, Gallacher, 1 o.g.)

Middlesbrough (a) lost 1–0.

1990–91: **Nottingham Forest** (a) lost 2–1 (Scott)

1991–92: **Tranmere Rovers** (a) draw 6–6 (Quinn 3, Peacock 2, Clark), lost on penalties.